blue
rider
press

yours for eternity

yours for eternity

a love story on death row

DAMIEN ECHOLS & LORRI DAVIS

BLUE RIDER PRESS

a member of Penguin Group (USA)

New York

blue
rider
press

Published by the Penguin Group
Penguin Group (USA) LLC
375 Hudson Street
New York, New York 10014

USA · Canada · UK · Ireland · Australia
New Zealand · India · South Africa · China

penguin.com
A Penguin Random House Company

Library of Congress Cataloging-in-Publication Data

Echols, Damien.
Yours for eternity : a love story on death row / Damien Echols, Lorri Davis.
pages   cm
ISBN 978-0-399-16619-8 (hardback)
1. Love.   2. Death row   3. Capital punishment.   4. Man-woman relationships.
5. Echols, Damien.   6. Davis, Lorri.   I. Davis, Lorri.   II. Title.
BF575.L8E365   2014   2014009058
364.66092—dc23
[B]

Printed in the United States of America
1   3   5   7   9   10   8   6   4   2

Book design by Claire Naylon Vaccaro

Penguin is committed to publishing works of quality and integrity. In that
spirit, we are proud to offer this book to our readers; however, the
story, the experiences, and the words are the authors' alone.

For Cally, Nicole, Jacob, Fran, and Capi
Our unsung heroes

Lorri Davis
20. 124 St.
N.Y.
11015

July 11, 1996

Dearest Lorri,

I was thinking about what you said about hating to have to go to work, and not being able to concentrate on it while you're there, and I've come to a conclusion. As soon as I am out, you have to quit your job, so we can leave and go to who knows where. Trust me, it'll be fun, and we'll have tons of strange, wonderful adventures. It'll be great, and you won't have to worry about going to a job you don't like. I will hear no argument on it. ☺ I'm dead serious, so I want you to agree to it. We'll meet all kinds of people, go anywhere we want, and not do anything that we don't want to (I'm not eating any vegetables). So what do you think? You have to say yes, because I'll just keep bugging you until you do. The first place we have to see is that town where you grew up, you have to show me everything. Then I'll show you West Memphis. After that, we can decide where to go by flipping a coin, or throwing darts at a map, or any other way we can think of. It'll be strange, and beautiful, and magick. What do you think?

Sending love forever to my dear one,

D.

Damien echoles SK 531
2501 State Farm Rd.
Tucker, Ark. 72168

NEW YORK NY 100
29 JUL 1996

Dieulo 7/00/96

One morning, about four o'clock, I was
driving my car just about as fast as I could.
I thought, "Why am I out on the highway
this time of night?" I was miserable, and
it all came to me: "I'm falling in love with
somebody I have no right to fall in love
with. I can't fall in love with this man, but
it's just like a ring of fire."

JUNE CARTER CASH

yours for eternity

authors' note

When we began our journey together, now nearly twenty years ago, we hadn't a clue what was in store for us. A young man on death row in Arkansas caught up in a terrible sequence of events and wrongful convictions. A woman in New York City who loved to go to the movies. Fate drew us inexplicably together—and we've spent the rest of our lives trying to explain the hows and whys of falling in love and building a life. There's no easy answer for why we wrote those first letters—why a young, successful woman writes a letter to a man in prison—and most especially why we kept on writing those letters. Except that the more we helped each other deal with pain and fear, the greater our hope for freedom and joy grew. There were terribly dark days, months, and years, and yet we survived—as many married people do, regardless of their circumstances. The moments of ecstasy, romance, humor, and companionship burned brighter for the obstacles we faced. Again, like any married couple has faced.

We wrote thousands and thousands of letters to each other between 1996 and 2011, when Damien was released. Sometimes five or six a day. It was a daunting task to reread and select the ones that best told our story, not to mention the occasional letter that we came across unopened—either one of us must have saved it to read later, and received a second or third letter that day and forgotten about it. We spoke too often to keep track. We didn't always date the letters, so we've gone by postmarks here rather than the day they were written, and some span the course of several days before they were mailed. We have hundreds of mailmen to thank for keeping our love alive, and for bringing us both the words we needed to live by every day.

Lorri Davis and
Damien Echols

April 1996

Dear Damien,

I really wanted to wait until you had a chance to reply to my letter (if you wanted to) before I bombarded you with another, but I have so many thoughts running through my head—I have decided to write them all down.

By the way—if I am encroaching on your privacy in any way—and you don't want me to write—please don't hesitate to let me know. Like I have mentioned already a few times—I don't know why I feel compelled to have contact with you—I just do—so I will write until you tell me to stop. I found an article in the *New Yorker* that you might find interesting—I don't know what your legal situation is—the film doesn't go into much detail about your appeal—what is happening? I have a friend whose father knows Kevin Doyle—I would like to make your case apparent to him—but only with your permission. I don't even know what would happen—but I figure the more people who know—the more will be done. I know the movie will help when it comes out—but in the meantime I will tell everyone I know about you.

How far away from West Memphis is Tucker? Do you get many visitors?

In the movie, your family and girlfriend (wife?)—that wasn't clear—she says you asked her to marry you—but that's all—they came across as very caring, compassionate people. I hope you have a lot of support from them. I hope you get to see your son. How long have you been incarcerated? What are your days like—do you share a cell with someone? Please excuse my ignorance, I just want a semblance of what your life is presently.

I hope it doesn't freak you out to have someone that you don't even know mooning over you so much. It kind of freaks me out that this is happening to me. I cry about it a lot. I am fortunate enough to have a job that allows me to listen to music and draw all day—but since I have become "acquainted" with you it's difficult—because I think about your situation all the time. I'm trying to figure out a positive way to deal with it. If I don't—well, I already have, right? I honestly believe that undying hope can do wonders in this world. Damien, I can't say that I believe in "God"; but something has brought you into my life, and as daunting as it is to me sometimes, I *know* it's a good thing.

I hope with all my heart you are O.K.

I am sending you a photograph of the place Father Damien had his colony on the island of Molokai. Isn't it beautiful? Such a beautiful place for such misery at one time.

The original *King Kong* was filmed on that rock in the center of the photograph.

That dark figure to the right is me. I was a little reluctant to send you a photograph of me—but I suppose it is only fair.

The graveyard has an empty grave where Father Damien was buried, but his body was eventually shipped back to Belgium.

O.K. I'll stop for now.

As I said before and will continue to say—let me know if I can send anything in particular to you. If you don't tell me I'm going to start sending you Danielle Steel novels and really nasty-smelling aftershave and sardines in mustard sauce, and pieces of red string that I find on the street, and last but certainly not least—a large pod of some sort.

I will, too.

Bye,

Lorri

April 1996

Dear Lorri,

Believe me, I in no way think that my privacy is being invaded and I do not mind being "bombarded with letters." I just sent off another letter to you a couple days ago, which you should have gotten right before this one. I can't remember if I enclosed those articles I was telling you about or not, so if I forgot, just remind me, and I'll get them out to you.

Thank you for the article from the *New Yorker*. I had read it a couple days before; I have a subscription to the *New Yorker*. I love the little cartoons they print.

I certainly don't mind you making my case known to Kevin Doyle. I would not object to anything that could possibly help.

Yes, I'm sure the film will convince a lot of people in other states of my innocence, but what worries me is whether or not the people of Arkansas will pay attention. They refuse to look at the evidence and they refuse to listen to reason. All they want is to see somebody die for those crimes and a "freak" like me is just as good as anyone. The whole attitude scares the hell out of me.

Thank you for telling everyone about me. Maybe if everyone were to take as big an interest as you have things could happen a lot faster. It just seems that most people just don't care, or they're so close-minded they won't even try to see the truth.

How far is West Memphis from Tucker? Exactly 147 miles. Yes, I usually have a visitor every week. My family and friends have really pulled together and they try to stay pretty close to me. They've been very supportive. No, unfortunately, I don't get to see my son. He'll be three years old this year, and I haven't seen him since he was about 5 months. My girlfriend moved to Arizona and took him with her. I haven't seen or heard from either of them since the trial. She's gone on with her life. I really can't blame her, I guess, since I've been locked up 3 years now. Maybe it's for the best, but it still hurts like hell.

My life? Well, I have my own cell, which I spend 22 hours a day inside of. I'm allowed to go outside for 2 hours a day, but I usually don't, because I'm not allowed around any of the other prisoners, and when you do go out, you just stand in a fenced square like a dog kennel and bake in the sun. I spend most of my time just lying on the bed listening to the radio and reading. There's absolutely nothing to do, but for some reason it still seems like time goes by incredibly fast. It's kind of hard to believe I've been here this long. It doesn't seem like it.

No, I don't believe in Christianity's version of God, either, but from the very beginning of this situation, I've felt that there had to be a purpose for all of this. Now I just have to figure out what the purpose is, so I can go home. ☺ Maybe this is just a way to pay off some karma I've built up in the past or something.

Thank you for the picture. Yes, it is beautiful. I hope to one day be able to go there for myself.

Why are you afraid for me to see what you look like? I'm not so shallow as to judge you by your physical appearance. Just relax and be natural. Trust me, we'll get along great.

I'm not sure that I'm in need of any Danielle Steel novels, nasty-smelling aftershave, bits of red string, or a pod of some sort, though I do appreciate the gesture. ☺ I can only have things made of paper. Remember, I am a dangerous lunatic. ☺

7

Right now, my first appeal hasn't even been heard yet. My case goes before the Arkansas Supreme Court on September second. We expect to be denied though. We don't expect to get any help until we reach federal court.

I guess I'm going to close for now, but I can't wait to hear from you again. You're a sweetie.

Forever,

Damien

postscript, 2014

When writing this book became a possibility for Damien and me, I felt myself immediately backpedaling into a place of fear, a place I haven't been in the past few years. I have been praying in the last year for all that I put into the world to be inspiring—whether I'm speaking with Damien at a public event or working privately on the WM3 case, which is still very much alive—and to help people believe in all they can do, that anything they can imagine is possible for them. This is the message that is most important to me, because it's how Damien and I came to live our lives while he was imprisoned. We credit this "magick," as we call it, with bringing about his freedom. And it is what enabled us to begin anew on August 19, 2011, to start over as a married couple finally living a life together, under one roof. But in looking back over our letters, I found myself being concerned about what people would think of me for sharing something so personal.

I think anyone would feel a sense of horror at having their most personal feelings laid out for the world to read. I have moments of panic thinking about it, but my hope that our story will inspire outweighs my fears. I have been approached many times over the years by people who ask how I kept going, or how did we keep our marriage alive while we were living in such dire circumstances. Perhaps this book will answer some of those questions, and hopefully help someone who is in a tough place.

The more I've thought about it, the more I've come to realize that these letters show the secret imaginations that guided Damien and me through all the things that we've accomplished—in our love, and in the world. We didn't know what was going to happen when we started writing to each other, but looking back it's uncanny how many things that we wrote about in those first letters actually became our reality.

These letters that cover a vast part of our eighteen years together are a gift to us both. I don't know many marriages that have a diary, a written record from the very beginning. While our circumstances were certainly not ordinary, the evolution and creativity in our courtship, and in our ongoing commitment to each other, are similar to what many people in lifelong relationships experience. It's universal. What I want to impart through our correspondence is that no matter what anyone may be going through, here's the thing: If you love each other, and if your relationship is worth the pain or the hardship, stay with it. The extraordinary treasure of sharing another person's life is one of the most gratifying experiences of being a human being.

Writing this book also gives Damien and me the opportunity to see again who we were and, in striking contrast, who we are now. Inside and outside of our marriage. Our relationship has been probed and questioned, and while we may not always have the answers, this is our side of the story.

Lorri Davis
New York, 2014

postscript, 2014

Looking back through these letters is like walking through a haunted house. In a lot of ways, I've tried to live my life with the motto "Don't look back." There are just too many ghosts following behind. Especially as I grow older. It seems like something happens every day to remind me that I'm not a young man. My steps aren't quite as certain as they were ten years ago. There are more strands of white in my hair and beard. And last night as we were getting off the bus, Lorri got her finger caught in the door and nearly broke it. It hurts my heart to see it today, the way it's swelling and turning black. Neither of us is as resilient as we once were. Looking back only reminds me of that even more.

Another thing I'm reminded of is how scared I was in the beginning. The reason I kept all of Lorri's letters at first was that I was scared that sooner or later she'd leave. That one day the letters would slow to a trickle, and then disappear altogether. I thought perhaps she'd meet someone else, someone she could actually touch, could fuck, could build a life with. Or that she'd realize how long and miserable the battle was that stretched out before her and decide it just wasn't worth it. I think that was because no one I'd ever known had ever stuck with me before. Sooner or later, every single person I'd ever known had either betrayed, left, or forgotten me. Every single friend, every family member, every lover. That was all I knew, and I didn't realize that life could be any other way. So I kept those letters, protected them as if they were the dearest treasure in the world, because part of me believed that one day they would be the only thing left of this beautiful and maddeningly magickal time of my life when I actually felt alive. I believed they would be all I had left of Lorri. I protected them like I was protecting my heart. Looking back I also see how I was never really even alive until I arrived on death row. I was beginning to be born on the day I was sentenced to death.

Another thing I realize in hindsight is how very little I ever wrote about the torture I was going through. These letters are completely void of the beatings, the starvation, and the psychological trauma I was enduring on a pretty regular basis. There are a couple of reasons for that. The first is that it played no part and had no place in the world we were creating together. And it was indeed a world that we were creating. Even though we were separated by space in the physical world, we were together in every other realm—the emotional, the mental, the astral, the etheric. The only part of us that wasn't joined together was our skin. Letter by letter, story by story, we were building a secret place that was far removed from daily prison life. We were building a packet of magick that became our refuge and sanctuary—and I did not want the horrors of my physical situation to seep into that place and corrupt it. I wanted to keep it as pure as I possibly could.

The other reason? Because I didn't want Lorri to have to carry that burden. Imagine the person you love most in all the world being tortured and abused right in front of you, and there being absolutely nothing you could do about it but sit and watch. The torture, pain, and humiliation isn't something that lasts an hour—or even a day. It's something that goes on year after year, with no end in sight and no way to change it. Having to witness something like that is the stuff that

Hell is made of—and there was no reason to heap that weight on top of everything else that Lorri was carrying. She was already carrying more than any human should ever have to.

Another interesting thing about looking back is how my understanding and practice of magick grew throughout the years. In my youth I viewed the practice of magick as something "special" and separate from the rest of life. It was something you broke out on special occasions, like Christians who only think of their god for an hour on Sunday. As more and more time passed, magick became part of my every waking moment. I eventually learned that we're doing magick all the time—most people are just doing it unconsciously. Over time I began doing magick nonstop. I'd begin doing it before I ever got out of bed in the morning, just to make the day go as smoothly as possible. I'd do it so that I could call Lorri on time, with as little interference from guards and malfunctioning phone lines as possible. If I lost or misplaced something, I'd do magick to find it. If I was being plagued by a particularly vile guard, I'd do magick to banish him from my life.

Then there was the ultimate goal of my freedom. The last year that I was in prison, I began doing magick for hours a day to secure my release. Within one year, freedom came to me like a sudden landslide.

Damien Echols
New York, 2014

April 10, 1996

Lorri,

Thank you so much for writing. I've been waiting. I knew that
sooner or later someone would take notice. You have no idea how
much it means to me for people to offer their support. You asked if
there was anything you could do to help. You've already helped
more than you know, just by writing. Thank you. Do you have any
idea how it feels to be called a killer by everyone who sees you, even
though you know you're innocent? I go through hell every day,
sitting here waiting to die for something I didn't do. It's a nightmare.

Thank you for the review of the film. I had heard about it, but
this was the first chance I've had to read it.

Yes, I have a way to listen to music. I have a radio that stays on
24 hours a day. Music has always touched me in ways that nothing
else can, the way some people are touched by art or poetry. I think
that if they took away my music, I would die. Music and reading are
pretty much what I live for at this point in time.

The way you described the place you grew up, I guess our
situations were pretty much the same. Even though everyone there
hated me, it was still my home. I loved the land, if not the people.
No matter where I moved, I always came back to West Memphis.

Yes, Father Damien's plight was something that really drew me,
amazed me, and interested me. I've always been amazed by people
who would spend their lives serving a cause, even though they knew
they would never be rewarded for it.

It seems that this film is beginning to turn things in my favor a little. There have been several small articles in various papers recently that seem to be pointing to my innocence. Every little bit helps.

There is also a book out now about my case, that's helping a little. It's called *The Blood of Innocents*. There's another one being written even now that should *really* help.

What do I think of the review? Well, it's better than some things that have been written about me. I'm not complaining.

Well, Lorri, I'm closing for now, but I truly hope to hear from you soon.

                                        Forever here,

                                                Damien

p.s. What did the other people who saw the film seem to think of it?

April 13, 1996

Damien,

I am so happy you wrote back. Now I can explain a little more
about the film and what happened afterward. First of all, I love
movies more than most things—but I'm pretty picky about what I
see. I don't see many documentaries—but a friend of mine had
tickets to *Paradise Lost*, and for some reason—I really wanted to see
it. The description in the film series program (New Directors/New
Films) did not prepare me for what I saw. Both directors were
present at the screening—and there were 400 people in the theater.
They had a question and answer session after the movie—and
everyone more or less voiced the same opinion—how could this
have happened? I, by that time, was already on my way to one of
the strangest of weeks I've ever experienced.

By the way, the questions most asked after the movie had
something to do with that knife—the audience found the whole case
ludicrous, and were amazed that a guilty verdict was delivered with
no evidence save that incredibly incompetent confession—which
wasn't even used in your case.

So . . . I came home that night and I couldn't sleep—I couldn't
stop thinking about your situation. It started getting increasingly
worse. I lost my appetite. It's all I could talk about.

Damien—now I'm prone to being maybe a bit obsessive, maybe a
bit too idealistic, definitely too sensitive—but I also think I'm pretty
realistic and level-headed. Well, something happened—my friends

thought I was losing my mind—all I knew was I couldn't stop thinking about you in that place—knowing—it was all so very wrong. I see and hear and read about injustices all the time. Unfortunately, I see people starving in the streets, here, I read about people dying for no reason. And yes, I hate it—but nothing has ever gotten through to me like you did. Maybe it's because you remind me a little of myself—I don't even know how, maybe growing up the way we did. I really can't explain it. One thing in my life that has never failed me is intuition or insight or being slightly psychic—call it what you want—but when something is so strong in my head—I know I must follow it. It didn't even occur to me to write to you for a few days. Then I decided I had to help you in any small way I could. It's something I really want to do.

So I'll start by sending you books. And since I don't know what you like to read, I'm sending you:

1. A book by my favorite writer—Julio Cortazar called *Cronopios and Famas*. J.C. can be very silly, but he's so magical. If you like this one—you'll like his other stuff because this is one of the most obscure of his books.
2. *Franny and Zooey* by J. D. Salinger—you've probably read this—but I keep this book wherever I go. Whenever I've been so sad that I can barely go on, I read this and it helps—so I hope it will help you.
3. *Heart of a Dog*—this book is just so funny to me. I think the writer is an ironic genius.

Please don't hesitate to tell me what you want to read. It's so easy to send books. As a matter of fact, I request that you send me a list of things. Do you like magazines?

Let me explain how I feel about this . . . it breaks my heart that you are where you are and you are forced to endure it—so I am committed to doing whatever I can to make your life a little more bearable—so don't hesitate to let me know if there is something you want.

By the way—your handwriting is so beautiful. Do you draw? I have a feeling you do. I feel a little more informed about you—I know it's not very fair. I know what you look like, what your temperament seems to be—you seem *very* composed and intelligent. It makes me feel a little sad—but what do you do—movies are like that. If you want to tell me more about yourself, please do. I'd be very interested. You just seem like a "true" person. I hope you know what I mean.

Damien, I promise I'm not a weirdo—(I was laughing when I wrote that).

I'm just following my heart on this one and I want to be a friend to you for as long as you want me to be—and maybe we really can become friends. If you haven't noticed, I love to write.

But, I will close for now.

Thank you for writing back to me.

Sincerely,

Lorri

P.S. I love to go back to West Virginia. I know what you were talking about—I love the land there—I love how quiet it is. One of my closest friends grew up in Arkansas—she calls the two places parallel universes! I've been to Arkansas—and I agree—the mountains are the same, the people, even the accent. My family still lives there and I go back as often as I can—but they don't really get me much there. Sometimes I feel stunted when I go there—verbally.

—Is it OK to send you packages?

—Do you have a Walkman or way to listen to tapes?

Bye for now,

Lorri

April 1996

Lorri,

   You have no idea how it made me feel when you said the
audience had a positive reaction to the film. I thought my heart was
going to burst. It gives me hope. Thank you so much.

   So, your friends thought you were losing your mind over this
case, huh? I just wish everyone could see the film and be as open-
minded as you were. Here in Arkansas, I'm a very hated person,
because everyone believes all they hear. They don't even bother to
look at the actual evidence, they just listen to rumors and gossip.

   I have beautiful handwriting? Thank you. No, I can't draw, even if
my life depended on it. Jason's the artist, I'm the poet. I'm sending
one of the latest things I've written, so be sure to tell me what you
think. I wrote it about two weeks ago.

   I saw my mother and father today. I love seeing them, but it
also hurts, because my mom always cries a lot. It tears me up inside
to see her do that, and know that there's absolutely nothing I can do
about it. It makes you feel so helpless.

Damien

April 23, 1996

Dear Damien,

When you write again, I know this is a lot to ask—but could you try to explain what your beliefs are? In the film your sister said that you at one time wanted to be a priest—but in your testimonies it seems you were delving into other beliefs. I am very interested in what you hold dear—or what you are devoted to. I am struck by the fact that you don't pretend—even with all that has happened to you—you don't present yourself in a false light. I have a great amount of respect for that. That aspect of you certainly came through in the film. I've never read much about the occult or wicka (sp?) although I have friends who know quite a bit about it—from the little I know—it seems a very early, mystical religion. I have always sought my own path with my life's belief—I was raised in a family of Southern Baptists, born-again Christians. No one could ever answer my questions—and they kept saying they loved everything and everyone on God's green earth—but they didn't.

I simply believe in love, hope, and fate. Simply put. I believe there are strong forces and if we don't go with them—our lives will be amiss of incredible experience. I've had some exceptional things happen to me—I liken it to magic. I believe very strongly in these forces—I don't even like to say "good" and "evil"—it's not that easy.

I know I have believed things into happening—sometimes it's scary—always wonderful—sometimes heartbreaking. I've met a couple of people who have had the same experiences—they know what I mean—it's very subtle, at the same time very intense.

So—I am believing in you with all my heart and soul. You need to be free—because I can tell your soul is full of murky, lovely, fascinating things. I know it when I see it or feel it, and I know you're a treasure.

Do you or can you keep in touch with Jason? How long have you been friends?

How often do your parents visit—or how often are you allowed visitors?

Maybe some day I can visit you—would they allow that? Could I bring you some kind of chocolate treat?

Surely, they'll let me.

Lorri

April 26, 1996

Dear Lorri,

My beliefs? Yes, at one time I very much wanted to be a priest. I
wanted to be a priest because for my entire life all I ever had were
questions that no one could ever answer. I wanted to know the
reason for my existence, and religion was the first logical place to
begin my search, but I still found no answers, so I got deeper and
deeper into the church. I thought maybe the priesthood would give
me a reason to live. I couldn't force myself to believe what the
church taught; there were just too many holes, which only brought
more questions. I began to look at other religions, searching for
something I could believe and put faith in, and that's how I became a
Wiccan. We believe in the creative force of life, which we call the
Mother Goddess. We believe in reincarnation and the ability to
shape our own destiny. It's one of the oldest surviving religions left
on the face of the earth. If you have any specific questions you want
to ask, I would be more than happy to answer them to the best of
my ability.

I agree with you about good and evil. I believe it is people who
make things good or evil. The powers of nature simply exist. It's up
to the individual to choose to use that force, and unfortunately,
some people use it for harm.

No, I definitely do not try to make myself appear as something
I'm not, or putting up a false front, because I believe that everything
you do eventually comes back to you—karma, which means that

people would eventually see through any false façade. It's far easier to simply present yourself as what you truly are.

I know what you mean when you said if you believe in something strong enough it will come true. I think everyone does it sometimes without even realizing it. Thank you for believing for and in me.

Well, I guess I'm going to close and get this in the mail, but I'll talk to you soon, and I can't wait to hear from you again.

Until then,

Forever,

Damien

May 1, 1996

Dear Damien:

Now we're going to be even more out of synch. Small bits of
each letter will start making sense, little by little. It's great, getting to
know someone by writing. It's quite wonderful and mysterious. I
like writing much better than the telephone. Although my closest
friend moved to Paris, so I like getting calls from her. She's another
one—like I have tried ever so ploddingly to explain to you. She
knows things. She has a magical thing in her—we knew as soon as
we met. We saw each other, we smiled, we linked arms and we
walked off—leaving everyone else to fend for themselves. She was in
NY at the time, then she moved to Boston—and then all the way to
France. I miss her something awful. But we see each other when we
can. She was a ballerina for the Boston Ballet—but she quit to
become a biologist. I like that, I hope some day to see her in a white
lab coat doing things—experiments and whatnot. Damien, if you
could study anything, what would it be? Are you obsessive (unlike
me—haha)? I'm incredibly so. As if you couldn't surmise—but I
think it's a trait worth having—I just have to watch it sometimes—
the combination of being obsessive and extremely emotional can
wreak havoc on everyday life.

Your parents must be so strong. Were they easy to grow up with?
Have they always accepted you? What are they like? My parents are
an odd combination. It's funny, I have 2 sisters; one older, one
younger (are you the oldest?). My sisters always were what my

parents wanted them to be—they were both homecoming queens!! But I was always doing something else—but no matter what I did— my parents hung in there with me—like when I was 3 I asked for a wig made of real hair, but it had to be white—like a horse's tail. Well, I don't know if it was real, but they got it for me, and I'm sure my mother was mighty embarrassed walking around in a supermarket with a three-year-old in that wig. I wore it all the time. Then when I was six, I asked for a suit (preferably pants and a vest) made out of snakeskin. I must have seen one somewhere, I don't know—but they got one for me (it was vinyl—but it looked like snakeskin). I got it in the summer—I wore it all the time, sweating. My parents are by no means "hip"—no, not at all—conservative as all get-out—but I think they like me—even though I've broken their hearts a million times.

I hope you don't mind rambling letters like this. Will you tell me some things you did as a child? The stories before the age of 10 are the best—I believe anything after that is merely a confirmation of everything that has already been formed.

Oh, Damien, I hope this letter finds you all right, and calm.

Thinking of you,

Lorri

postscript, 2014

I grew up in a small town in West Virginia. My family wasn't wealthy. I was the middle child of three daughters born to parents who loved each other—had actually been together since they were in high school. My sisters and I grew up playing fantasy games. Our imaginations ran rampant, and what I recall most from my childhood is silliness and make-believe. We bought into all the fairy tales. We read books, and we dreamed, and we grew up happy.

So as I grew older, I knew I wanted to live an adventurous life. I didn't know that that could mean pain, but I've always known that I wanted to conquer fear. My fears lay mostly in dealing with people and, strangely enough, logistics. I would force myself to speak in front of a class, travel alone or talk to strangers. I wouldn't even want to do something as simple as order takeout. So anything I could do to be fearless, I wanted to do it.

During college I was intent on studying landscape architecture in England. I had always loved the gardens and architecture there, and found the idea of living in the English countryside just about the most romantic thing I could imagine. We didn't have the money for anything so exotic, but we managed it somehow. After that experience, I never looked back. I knew that I would never settle down into a "normal" life, and that whatever I wanted, I would find a way to get it.

I lived in London for a while, then Ohio, where I married a musician named David. We didn't make it as a couple but we're still friends, and I credit him with the start of a very important chapter of my life: New York. If I hadn't been so distraught over our breakup, I wouldn't have been driven to move there with very little money and a wish for something new and exciting.

I lived in New York for ten years. I was very happy, and I built a successful life there. My career as a landscape architect was all I had ever hoped for—I worked for some extraordinary firms and partnered with some amazing clients. Some of the estates I helped design included those of Carolyne Roehm and Henry Kravis, the Pritzkers, and Oscar de la Renta. My work for the City of New York included jobs for the Metropolitan Museum of Art, City Center, and Lincoln Center. I truly felt at that point I was living the grown-up version of a fantasy life. I was moving about in a world of the super-privileged, and my life was fun.

I had very dear friends, including a ballerina from the Boston Ballet and two of the most talented, kind, and wise women I've ever known. I met Sherri almost immediately after arriving in New York, and we spent time together there and in Boston. We saw films, read the same books, and were always up for an adventure. I worked with Susan and Shelley at a design firm in Soho. Susan and I went on to live next to each other when I moved to Brooklyn. We shared a great deal of each other's lives. Shelley was always my rock. All three of them are still in my life and were a great source of support to me over the years in Arkansas.

My charmed existence in New York came to a screeching halt in February 1996, when I walked into the Museum of Modern Art to see a film called *Paradise Lost*. To say I was moved by the story is an understatement. Like all the other New Yorkers around me, I was aghast at what I was seeing on the screen. Unlike most of the other audience members, I was from the South. I understood the culture that was being represented by the people in the documentary. I grew up attending a fundamentalist Baptist church. The Bible Belt was the backdrop of my childhood. Seeing Damien demonized was not so shocking to me, though I felt terrible pain for him.

From the moment I saw Damien, I felt a kinship with him. There was something in him that I recognized. He was definitely a product of his community, yet he wanted something else. He was different, and it was that difference that invited the horror that became his life. Unlike me, able to move about and make my own choices, he was caught, literally, and held captive for what he believed in, and that weighed heavily on my heart.

So much so that I couldn't get him out of my mind. I grieved for him, and it affected my daily life. I heard a voice deep inside telling me that I needed to help him, and it wasn't until I finally decided to write to him that I felt any relief in my heart. I reached out to him as a friend, as someone who might help him. And I felt a huge responsibility, even in that first letter. I didn't want him to feel that I was a spectator, gawking at him, or a rubbernecker. I just wanted to help him in some way, but only if he told me there was something I could indeed do to help.

I'll never forget seeing his first letter on the floor under the letter slot in my front door. I was elated, and scared at the same time. A combination of feelings I would come to know very well over the next couple of decades. Its arrival coincided with the first and only visit to New

York by my parents. I carried it around in my pocket all day before finally getting a moment of solitude to read it late that night.

After reading his first letter, I was compelled to write back, and I never questioned that I would continue to write to him. I suspended all of the niggling questions my mind should have been asking, such as, "He is in such a vulnerable position, what if you let him down or hurt him?" But from the moment I wrote to Damien, it felt natural for me to be doing so. One letter followed the next, and in no time, we were obsessed with getting to know each other. We held no judgment toward each other. It was one of the most joyous, reckless, amazingly alive times in my life, and yet it was undercut with a sadness and grief that I couldn't get out from under.

Lorri

May 2, 1996

Dear Damien:

I've just been out walking in the streets. I mailed a book to you.
Sometimes I wish I could talk to you. You know, sit and talk for a
long time. But then I think this is one of the nicest things I've ever
done—get to know someone without ever speaking to them—it's
like a wonderful spell. Although, I think we'll see each other
someday, and definitely hear each other's voices at some point.
There's a sort of freedom in just writing. What do you think?

I love the night. When I was growing up, I used to crawl out of
my window and just walk around by myself. From like 2:00 a.m. to
5:00 a.m. was the best. There were all these fields around my house
and I'd look into people's windows. No one ever knew where I was
or what I was doing out there. Then I would sleep till 12:00 noon. I
love being places where no one knows where I am, like in an attic. I
like to get away with things, like following someone for a few
hours—wherever they go. That's fun. Once I ended up on a train to
upstate NY! But I would never want to talk to these people. Just
watch them. I really don't think they'd mind. I wouldn't mind if
someone watched me for a while then disappeared forever. I think
it's kind of sweet. I don't know what it is that makes me want to
follow certain people. Sometimes I see them and my breath gets
taken away for a second. It has nothing to do with physical looks—
beauty, clothes, or stature—it's something else, something striking—
or dark or "off."

Oh! How I wish I could make you happy—even for a little while.

Please tell me anything possible that I can do that will make you happy. Even gleeful.

I have never taken a drink of alcohol in my life, nor have I ever taken any drugs—but I suppose many things are drugs—coffee, sex, sugar—so I don't know if that statement is true. I have nothing against alcohol or drugs—au contraire—I find them quite fascinating and I am forever asking my friends about them—especially psychedelic drugs. When I was 10 years old—I made some rules for my life and those rules included I never wanted to drink or lose control of my mind in the state that I know it by chemical inducement. I can't even tell you why. All I know is that I've never even been tempted. The other rule was that I was to live without guilt. That one has been more difficult—but I do fairly well. I trust myself enough to know that if I want to do something or don't want to do something—I have to go on my instinct. I suppose the hard part is when someone's feelings are in danger of being hurt. That's when I have problems.

I am home, now. I'm in Clay, West Virginia, where my father grew up. We are staying in the house he grew up in—a very simple wood-frame house.

My father was dreadfully poor growing up—he had 8 brothers and sisters and this house has only 3 rooms. They didn't have running water or electricity at all, then my dad's mother died while giving birth to his younger sister when my father was 2 years old, so he doesn't remember her. My dad said he was always scared growing up—because there wasn't anyone to take care of him except his older sisters. He said he ate cornflakes almost all of the time and sometimes for Christmas he would get blackberry ice cream. But he grew up into such a kind-hearted man—but I know he still harbors fear in his heart. My parents honestly don't know what to make of me. I always feel so alone when I come home. This time I've come home for a family reunion that we have every year. We hang out in the graveyard for most of the time—having a picnic and talking. Although no one really knows what to say to me—I've always been really quiet around them. Last year someone called me a kite without a string (!?).

In the last week, my thinking has radically changed. I'm starting to realize things about myself that I never have. It feels like the world is a new place for me these last few days—and this is all because of you. Because of you, my life is going to change.

Do you like maps? I love them—I tried to find Tucker on a map—but couldn't find it—I'll have to get a better map. I did however find West Memphis. I drove all over Arkansas, but I didn't drive through West Memphis. I had an idea today—I don't know if you would want to do it—but it may be fun. On the next full moon—which will be July 1st, at 11:00 pm we start writing to each other and we write down any thought that comes into our heads—it doesn't matter what they are or if they even make sense—just a stream of consciousness. What do you think? And then we mail it the next day without rereading it! I wonder what would happen? Let me know if you want to. Maybe it's too silly.

But I kind of think it's fun.

Oh, yes—maps. When I was in Turkey last October—we drove all over that country—in a teeny red car—we kept getting pulled over by the police—at check areas along the road—we found out later they were looking for 2 terrorists in a red car traveling somewhere in western Turkey. I had a gun pulled on me twice—both by cops—right in my face—it's funny, I didn't even flinch. I don't even know why, because Turkey is wild. You just don't know what is going to happen to you there—I loved it—you hear horrible things about Turkish prisons and all—but look what's happening in Tucker, Arkansas. Americans just don't seem to realize what's going on under their own noses.

Do you love full moons? I do. I get so crazy with it. Absolutely, wonderfully insane. Does anything happen to you?? And water. I suppose swimming during a full moon is my favorite thing to do. I don't get to do that much. Not here.

There is a man in Ohio that I got to be friends with—he's a very eccentric man and I took to him immediately. Well . . . not immediately. During one of our first meetings I was barefoot and he took my foot and began licking my toes, so on and so on. I was very calm and fixed him with a special eye and said, "Stuart, don't do that!" He stopped—he said he liked women who were up-front with him (?!). Anyway, we became friends. Two years later he almost died from an illness—it was terribly hard on him—but he lived! And he said he wanted to travel the world and not waste what he had (he's very wealthy—well, moderately wealthy)—and he wanted me to always travel with him. So after a while, I decided to—so (this story is coming full circle, I promise) I've been to some incredible places, mysterious ancient places like Turkey and Marrakesh and Greece— but Stuart lets us travel on the full moon so I can swim in the sea by myself at night. I have no fear of water at all.

I am scared of some things—some people—some places—but I'm still intrigued with fear. It's essential. I want to poke and prod it. For some reason—I am afraid of my teeth being smashed into my gums. So I'm careful walking up stairs and around baseballs and such.

I'll be thinking of you till next time,

Lorri

May 6, 1996

Dear Lorri,

Of course I will read *Hopscotch*. You said it's your very favorite book, and I am curious to see why you love it. Actually, I guess I'm more curious about you, and maybe I can gain a better insight on you by looking at things you hold close or dear. I think I have a little better "feel" on you now. You seem exotic to me. I mean, you love classical music, you like "real" movies not just "splatter films" like most people I know, and the books you read have "class" and "culture." You seem like a very gentle soul, caring and educated. It's very beautiful, but at the same time it makes me feel like such a redneck. My friend Rick from New Orleans says I'm not a redneck, I'm a "southern gentleman," but I still feel like nothing more than a redneck.

You've lost 5 pounds due to worrying about me? You've got to stop that, I'm fine. I actually feel a little better lately. Most people spend their entire lives running from themselves. But when you're locked in a small room all alone for a few years, you have no choice but to face yourself, and stare down the truth, and look into the face of your "inner demons." Then, either you overcome them, or they overcome you. There are only two possible outcomes—either you find some sense of inner peace, or you go down a long, lonely path of self-destruction. I won't say that I don't still have my bad days, because I do, but I think that for the most part, I'm at peace with myself. There's no longer a war going on inside my head.

I'm including a visitation form in this envelope, in case you're ever down this way. Just fill it out and send it to the address at the bottom, and I'll let you know as soon as it is approved. One day, hopefully, maybe I'll even be able to come visit you. You could show me around. New York is one of the few places I've never lived. I've always wanted to see the Chelsea Hotel, which is supposed to be haunted by Sid Vicious and Janis Joplin.

Well, I guess I'm going to close up for now, but I can't wait to hear from you again. I love hearing from you.

Forever here,

Damien

May 5, 1996

Dear Damien,

You know, I shaved my head after a devastating relationship, too. And like you, the pain almost killed me. Instead of walking in the sun, I would drive in my car for hours and days, pull off, sleep, hardly knowing where I was. This went on for weeks. That kind of pain is like no other. It's because of that situation that I ended up in New York. It was the hardest thing I could think of to do—I didn't know anyone here, I had no place to live, and very little money. It worked, though.

I believe in reincarnation, sometimes; however, it is very, very difficult to see things from a broader perspective—I mean over time—and lives that we have no memory of—learning from past mistakes and triumphs. In some ways, it makes some moments in life bearable. It's the only reason I've been able to understand or accept this strong feeling I have for you—for your well-being. It's one of the most bizarre things that I've ever felt—but at the same time, perfectly natural. I felt like I knew you after that movie. Even as if we had talked before. And even though it has made me into a weepy woman—nobody knows what's wrong with me—Damien, I'm glad it's happened.

You are incredibly inspiring.

OK, I'm going to stop for now. I feel as if I could write you every day. I feel as though I have so much to tell you.

Most of it is pretty silly—I really try not to overwhelm you with my prattling away.

But if you want to hear stories—let me know.

I can't wait to hear from you.

Your friend,

Lorri

May 3, 1996

Dear Lorri,

The relationship you have with your friend from Paris sounds
wonderful. I have a friend kind of like that. As soon as we saw each
other, it was like, "Even though I've never met you, I know you!" It
is a great experience.

Yes, I am also very obsessive. Once I become attached to
something, it's like I can never truly walk away from it. I tend to
keep it very close to my heart forever.

My parents? Actually, I never got a chance to know my father
during childhood. I never knew him. We have just started to
communicate over the past 4 or 5 years. It's a strange experience
when you're meeting your father and he has to ask you who you
are. I was raised by my mother and grandmother for the most part.
They would do anything to help me, and my grandmother always
looked at me as if I were an angel. I was very close to my
grandmother, and when she died 2 years ago, it tore me apart. I
couldn't even go to the funeral. Yep, I'm the oldest. I have a sister
who is 19 and a half brother who is 10.

If I could study anything, what would it be? All the world
religions. That's what occupies my time now. I read everything I can
get my hands on, especially reincarnation and meditation. I found
that at their core, all religions teach the same principles. You
mentioned reincarnation in your last letter. If you stop and think
about it, it's the only reasonable explanation for a lot of things, like

different types and classes of people, why some live in poverty while others are rich, etc. Or people who have phobias—like being buried alive or drowning or high places.

I laughed when I read about your white wig. I could see it as plain as day in my mind, and it was hilarious. ☺ When I was young, I was obsessed with cowboys. Everywhere I went, I wore my hat and guns, and I wouldn't even look at the television unless it was a Gene Autry or Roy Rogers movie. I was also horrified of taking baths, because I was positive I would go down the drain. My mom used to have to fight me to get me into the bathtub, because I would be kicking and screaming. We also had a Dixie cup dispenser in the bathroom, and I would lock the bathroom door and use all the Dixie cups to drink water out of the toilet because we thought it "exciting."

I also used to think I was really loved, but the longer I'm here, the more people drift away and forget me. Oh well, now at least I know who my true friends are.

I don't think you "prattle away." You keep me company. Yes, I would love to hear stories. I'm interested in your life. It's like I said before, you seem exotic.

Trust me, my entire life is out of sync, so why should our letters be any different? ☺

The way you described how you felt after a bad relationship hit me close to home. I know exactly how you felt, because I was in complete agony. The end of that relationship was the most devastating, miserable thing I'd ever felt in my life, and there was absolutely nothing I could do about it. No amount of physical pain could ever amount to that burden of emotional pain. There's no way to describe how it hurt. It took me a few years to get over it.

Well, I guess I'm going to close up for now and go take a shower. It's been a couple of days, so I guess I need one. ☺ I can't wait to hear from you. I'll be here waiting.

Your friend,

Damien

May 1996

Dear Damien:

I have told my friends about you, as you already know, so I was telling my very close friend Susan—she lives in the apartment above me . . . that you can only receive paper. Friday evening I was reading a letter that had just arrived from you—and she said—Oh! I have a present for him! So she pulled this out of her bag (the paper thing enclosed). It's from Chinatown and you have to blow it up. I thought it was so sweet that she was thinking about you and got it. Susan is the best. I think the thing that makes me happiest in life is that I have been blessed with the sweetest people around me. People with hearts of pure gold.

It is so funny right now—here I am—on the grass—drinking water with my cat—the neighbors to the left are playing basketball—loudly—and the ball keeps coming into our garden—the neighbor to the right is sitting outside strumming a guitar (nicely). The neighbor in front is playing Dominican music. And my head is miraculously clear.

Damien, will you tell me one of your favorite memories?

Thinking of you,

Lorri

May 14, 1996

Dear Lorri,

One of my favorite memories? Well, when I was 16 years old, I was very much in love. Her name was Deanna. One day we skipped school together. We walked for miles until we found a place that was absolutely beautiful. There were hills, and the grass was so full and soft and green, the sky was grey and overcast. We spent hours talking, telling each other things that we had never told another living soul, our worst fears, our most wished-for dreams, and we made love several times. I never suspected that that would be the last time I ever saw her. There's no way that words can ever do this memory justice, but it's a day that has returned to haunt me every day of my life.

Friends forever,

D.

May 1996

Dearest Damien,

There is no doubt in my mind that you are a very strong part of my past. No doubt. All I had to do was see you, hear you speak—and I was gone. Literally. Some door opened in my head and all I knew was—"You have got to locate this person—contact him—it is crucial." I was so scared you weren't going to receive my letters. I know this is real—nothing in my life has been quite so real.

It's funny, what you said about wondering what I do at night—every night (I usually go to sleep at 12:00 or so) I whisper good night to you and wonder what you are doing! I sometimes hope you can feel me thinking of you—but I've never tried thought transfer.

Does NY scare me? Well, really—no. I feel so strong here sometimes. No one even looks at you funny. I feel completely accepted. Sometimes I let the hair grow on my legs and under my arms and no one even looks—when I was in West Virginia last week, everyone looked. I can't stand that. New York after a while is very accepting. It's exciting, too. But at the same time—it's perfectly possible to live a "quiet" life.

I know I've asked you already so if you don't want to tell me—say, "Lorri—I'm just not going to tell you."

But . . . when is your birthday? Mine is July 16th.

I have grey eyes and I weigh 120 pounds and stand 5′6″. My hair is brown. I'm prone to freckles—have no birthmarks and am extremely fair.

There.

Affectionately,

Lorri

May 21, 1996

Dear Lorri,

   With everyone who I ever become close to, I leave part of myself with them, and I carry part of them with me. I find it to be a very beautiful, if slightly weird, experience. I guess you can tell my hands are shaking now, my writing is not too good. This is along the lines of what I was trying to say in my last letter, about meaningful conversations, and examining each other's thoughts, ideas, love, fears, and dreams.

   Just relax and let things flow. Some memories stay with us all our lives.

   Yes, the full moon makes me feel wonderful. When I am out on those nights, I can hardly even stand to wear clothes. I just want to strip down to my bare skin, and throw my head back and laugh with the pure joy of being alive. It would make me want to just run and run and run, just celebrating and wallowing in the fact that I existed.

   I also used to do like you, I would sneak out, and sometimes I would go to the lake near my house and just sit silently watching the moonlight reflection on the water. Sometimes, I would also lie on a hill watching all the cars speeding over the overpass, thinking about where they were going, smiling to myself over the fact that they never even knew they were being watched. My favorite time was when it was so cold that I could see my breath. I love the cold. To me, there is no such thing as "too cold."

   I never looked in anyone's windows, but I used to go to a store a couple miles away from my house that was open 24 hours a day, where I would perch on top of a garbage can and just watch everyone coming and going. I've always thought human beings were the strangest, most beautiful creatures. Once I even told my mom what I had been doing and she wouldn't believe me, because she said there was no way that someone could squeeze through the tiny window in my bedroom (it was really tiny).

I always went alone, because I knew no one else would understand. They would have asked questions like, "How long do we have to just sit here?" Or "Why are we doing this?"

What am I afraid of? The only thing I can think of that I am scared of is the same thing I'm attracted to—people! Sometimes they can be so cold, cruel, and mean, and it really hurts me. It's worse than physical pain.

Your friend forever,

Damien

June 14, 1996

Dearest Lorri,

Did you see *Good Morning America*? It was great! I know you said
you don't want to hear anything else about me from the media, but
it's so wonderful down here now. Everyone is talking about it, and
they believe me! It's beyond words, it's just too perfect. Our lawyers
were even on the radio this morning, and everyone who called in
was supporting us! It's such a change, I can't even believe it.

Also, some of the guards just came to my door talking about
Paradise Lost. They believe me! They believe I'm innocent and they
said all of Arkansas was saying the same thing! This is so great. They
were also laughing, because they said if someone saw the film, and
then looked at me, they wouldn't recognize me. I asked them, "Why
not?" and they said because in the movie I looked fat and bigger
than I am, and I had short hair. One of them said, "Now you look
like a bushman, you're as skinny as a stick, and you've got hair
halfway down your back." Lorri, this is so great. I knew something
like this would happen, but I still wasn't prepared for it. It's so
overwhelming.

You really, really shocked me when you said that you were
once married. The story about you and David, in a way it was
very beautiful, but it was also so sad. I know the pain he feels, he
still loves you so much that it hurts, but I also know how you felt,
it's like you said—you had to have him completely or not at all.
Yes, it's like you said—those feelings can be so very beautiful, but

they're always so painful. It's like being in heaven and hell at the same time.

Yes, I know what you mean about communicating like this, and it is wonderful. It's sort of like both of us is pure thought, we have no form, just like two energy forms who meet to exchange thoughts, emotions, feelings, ideas, and information, only to discover that they are really extensions of each other, always connected, but just beginning to realize it. I've been thinking constantly now. You know the book you sent, *The Holy Kaballah*? Well, people who have made really in-depth studies of it say that it teaches that before a soul is born into the flesh, it is whole and complete—neither male nor female—then when it's ready to be reborn in the flesh, it is split in half—male and female—and born into 2 bodies. Maybe that's the case of you and me, maybe we were once "one." I don't know, but it would describe the way you explained how you think of me— neither young or old, male or female, just part of "us."

I got a letter from my mom, and she said she's thinking of moving to Tennessee, up in the hills away from everything and everyone. She says she feels really at peace up there, with nothing to distract her. I envy her. Anyway, she wants to know my opinion. I know it's the best thing for her, but she already feels so far away, and she would be even farther. Why does everything always have to change? Why does nothing ever stay the same? I know that even I can't stay in West Memphis forever, I have to move on, but I will miss it, and it will hurt to leave. I don't know where I will go, I just know I'll have to go west. I'll stick a few things in a backpack and go until I find somewhere that feels right.

Sending much love forever,

Damien

June 17, 1996

Dear Sweetest Damien:

I have just received your letter telling me of the positive reactions to *Paradise Lost*. I am so, so happy. Believe me, I want to see all the media in the world that will tell the world of your innocence or will change some minds and get you out of there. Oh, it's such a good thing. I am so thankful that the movie was made. I knew it was going to help—I have a feeling it's just the beginning. When you get out, I'm going to take you to Ireland as a celebration gift!! Wouldn't that be great?!

But Damien, please, please try to eat. Please, I can't tell you how I began to cry so hard when I read that you only drink tea! You have to eat every day—you have to start. I know I sound like a mother hen, but if it helps any, think every day, "I'll eat today for Lorri." I mean it. You wrote in a letter recently about repaying me—and I scoffed at it—but now I know how you can "repay" me: Just eat. Try to keep yourself healthy. I know it's hard—I know your life is hell right now. I know I write a lot of nonsense about bugs or worms or whatever, but I never forget where you are and how little I know about what you're going through. It's only when sometimes you tell me something like you weigh less than 120 pounds and you can't eat solid food that I swing back to know you are hurting so badly and I feel so helpless. It makes me crazy sometimes. Please tell me you will try.

You asked why things always have to change. I've asked myself that question a million times, and it doesn't do any good—but I've learned that—you know, I don't know what I've learned from it—sometimes it just plain hurts—but I've changed so much since I've met you—in the most incredible way—you have affected my life—in ways I have not yet begun to explain to you—but I will, in time.

I know I've said it before and all the time, but you mean more to me every day and I will never leave you, never, no matter where you are.

I have to tell you that I couldn't write to you right away—I was crying so much—and Susan came downstairs and told me—I had been telling her about how sometimes I just send these terribly silly or edgy letters to you—like you were living in Palookaville, you know, driving round in a car or something. I was so shaken and sad—because you're not. Susan made me feel better. She said that when she was really sad (for about a year) she was heartbroken—she used to come downstairs to hear me ramble on about, well, you know how I go on about things. She said it made her feel like there was something else to fill her head with for a little while. Something that didn't hurt—it might make her nauseous, but not sad.

You needn't respond to that.

Just know that I am aware of your pain, I can never imagine the depth, but I know it's there—and I will spend my life trying to lessen it in any small way I can.

Please eat. OK??

Damien, I truly care for you so very much.

Yours, Lorri

June 17, 1996

Dearest Lorri,

Relax, sweetie, I know how you feel, I know what you mean.
Words sometimes feel so useless, because they're such small trivial
things, and they can't come anywhere close to explaining or
describing the huge, intense emotions you feel. The word "emotion"
doesn't even begin to describe your feelings, because it's so very
much more powerful than the word "emotion" can mean. You don't
even have to try to explain unless you want to, because I can feel it.
There's no need to try to explain unless it makes you feel better.

The word "love" is too small to encompass all that you feel. No
word will fit. At least no word that the human tongue is capable of
producing. The only way I know to let you know that I experience
the same thing is by telling you this—the only way to let you know
how strongly it has affected me is by telling you what I almost did
the other day. I have become friends with the man and woman who
did a lot of the work for *Paradise Lost*. Their names are Burk and
Kathy. Anyway, for the past month, they have been doing everything
in their power to get me released. Anyway, they've been in charge of
a lot of other films, too, including *From Dusk till Dawn*, *Even Cowgirls
Get the Blues*, and *Hellraiser III* and *IV*. Well, I was talking to Burk and
he said that they had been placing a lot of bets with people as to
how soon I would be released, and he said that as soon as I am free,
he wants me to come to Los Angeles, because he and Kathy could
use me in a lot of their films. (I would actually be a movie star. ☺)

Well, the first thing that almost rolled off my tongue was, "I can't move that far away from Lorri." I caught myself, and I was kind of confused, because I knew he would have no idea what I was talking about, or even who "Lorri" was. So what I said was, "Sure, I'd absolutely love to." But I knew that there was no way I could live on the complete opposite side of the country as you, because I feel I have to stay close to you.

I understand, and I know. It would be impossible for it to be some type of physical thing, because neither of us even really knows what the other looks like. We have a general idea, but that's it. In a way, I feel that it would be better if neither of us even had bodies. I can't explain what I mean by that. It would be impossible. Once again, "words won't do it."

It's just so intense, like you and I are both so much more, and so much bigger than these small shells of flesh can contain. Sometimes, every once in a while, I feel like I am you. I can recognize these times because I feel so innocent, as if I am looking at the universe through childlike eyes. Sometimes it's like I know that if my physical body were to change and conform to what it houses, I would appear as an impossibly old man, withered and eroded, but still nowhere close to death. But you seem so young and strong and beautiful. Never mind, I better stop before I get too weird for myself to understand. It just flows out of my mind and into my hand, onto the paper.

Sending love forever to my dear one,

D.

June 18, 1996

Dearest Lorri,

I just got both of your letters. I kind of embarrassed myself. When the mailman came in, I was hopping from foot to foot with impatience. He handed me an armload of mail (you wouldn't believe all of it!) and I started throwing stuff in every direction, looking for anything from you. The mailman just looked at me as if I were a lunatic. Oh well, they all think I'm crazy anyway.

*

I know, I'll be so glad when you can come here, too. I don't think you'll pass out, but if you do, it's nothing to be upset over. I was trying as hard as I could to keep from fainting when the jury said, "Guilty, guilty, guilty," but it only lasted for a second, then it was replaced by a feeling of calmness deeper than anything I've ever felt. Even then, I knew it was going to work itself out.

Oh, Lorri, you wouldn't believe the reaction the film has gotten. I know I'll be leaving here soon, and I can feel a path opening before me. I feel so excited, yet peaceful at the same time.

Yes, I did know that I was above everything, and that no one could touch me, but sometimes it's painful to know it. Sometimes it makes me feel so alone, even in a room full of people. Sometimes it makes me feel so very old, as if I'm the only adult surrounded by infants. Sometimes I would give anything to just be "one of the guys." But at other times I wouldn't want to be anything other than what I am, not for anything in the world.

*

I'm lying here now listening to people on the radio talk about me. It's so strange, I don't think I'll ever get used to that. Sometimes I have to shut it all out, it's so overwhelming. It makes my head hurt. They even dedicated two songs to me. Wow! It's going to take time to take this all in. Sometimes it scares me.

Sending love forever to my dear one,

Damien

June 25, 1996

My Dearest Lorri,

You have to stop worrying so much. Remember, I haven't lived this long without doing something right. ☺ Me being here is not the reason I can't eat; it's because I have ulcers and most food hurts me. I have to be careful because I don't know what will and won't hurt after I eat it. I've always loved cereal, but the other day I wasn't thinking and I ate some Raisin Bran. PAIN!! I was in agony for 3 hours. I couldn't even stand up. I eat a lot of bread, because it's easy on me. Yes, Lorri, I will eat more, just stop worrying. Man, I should have never told you that. ☺

I don't want you to stop talking about the things you talk about. I absolutely love the way your mind works. I don't want to sit around thinking and talking about this place all the time. Most of the time, it's the farthest thing from my mind. It's really not so bad here. I have plenty of solitude, which I love. Just relax, sweetie, everything's fine, OK? I'll be free soon anyway. ☺ Lorri, please don't cry. Don't you know that when you do that, you hurt me, too? You have to stop, for me. Everything's going to be OK soon, and we'll never have to think about bad things again. Just wait and see. It's going to be great.

You needn't ever hold your feelings, thoughts, or anything else back. Just let it flow. Trust me. ☺

Sending much love forever to my dear one,

Damien

June 1996

Dearest Lorri,

I would love to be able to talk to you on the phone, but I can't call until next month, because we're only allowed to change phone numbers 3 times a year, and I can't change them until the first week of July. I would absolutely love to talk to you.*

I know what you mean about seeming like I'm older. Then again, I feel like I'm older than dirt most of the time. For some reason, though, it does seem like you're younger. I feel a very protective urge toward you, like you're so fragile, and I want to cover and protect you to make sure you don't break. It's not exactly like a "big brother" feeling, but it's close to it. Am I making any sense?

Sending much love,

Damien

---

* I was only allowed to have three phone numbers on a list of people allowed to call the prison, and it often took months to change those numbers.—DE

June 27, 1996

My dearest Damien:

Today, I find myself thinking only of you. It's been one of those days when I miss you so much. I keep having to look up at the ceiling to keep from dropping tears on this drawing I am working on.

*

Oh Damien, will this ever get easier? I sometimes am amazed at how people can walk around with such pain and longing in their hearts. How can people who are somehow a part of each other live their lives apart? How do they walk around day after day with gaping holes in themselves? How do they continue to get up, do the mundane things like cross the street, drink a glass of water—let alone the extraordinary things such as read a letter, hear music, or have their breath stolen from them?

Time keeps going on, doesn't it?

I keep asking these questions daily—I keep looking for clues or evidence—and I don't know why because I am living proof!

I would endure it forever if it means having any part of you as part of me.

It's true, I feel better when you tell me to relax. Sometimes, however—this all gets the better of me, and this is the only thing that helps, to write to you, to share my thoughts with you.

Sometimes I fear the fact that the life I have had is slipping away from me—eroding slowly. I do sometimes fear for my sanity—even though in my heart of hearts I know it's intact. This is the way I need to be right now—I need to feel all of this, I need to close everything else out for a while, let things fall away from me—only then will I know what it will be or what it means.

*

I love you, Damien.

    You mustn't ever doubt it.

Bye for now.

Yours, Lorri

June 1996

Dearest Lorri,

The way your mind works is so delightful to me, it makes me smile from the wonder of it—chastity belts, 17-year locusts, it's wonderful. You made me smile on a day that has been filled with the purest horror I've ever witnessed, but I'll get to that later, I don't want to think of it for now.

*

I know what you mean about wanting to know everything all at once, but I also love the way the mysteries unfold a layer at a time, holding you spellbound with the pure beauty of it. I don't think we could fully appreciate life if things were revealed to us all at once. We need time to fully examine things, to "let them sink in," as you say. Sometimes I spend ages contemplating the simplest things. I like to examine everything from every angle.

Yes, I suppose some pretty devastating things have happened to me, but I've discovered something—that even when I was in the deepest depths of misery and despair, I was still in love and enchanted with the simple fact of my existence. It just seems so wonderful that I'm actually in this body, able to live and love, surrounded by so many beautiful souls, so much to do, so much to experience. It's all so wonderful. I also realize that if I wouldn't have been through the horrid, ugly, brutal experiences I've been placed in, then I would never have been able to recognize beauty, because I would have nothing to compare it to.

*

Yes, let's both write down our thoughts on the night of the full moon. I think it's a wonderful idea.

*

You've been approved to come see me if you're ever down this way. I can't wait to hear from you again, you mean a lot to me.

Sending much love,

Damien

P.S. Don't worry about losing me again, I'm here to stay this time. ☺

July 1, 1996

Dearest Damien,

You say you like the way my mind works—well, I think your mind is incredible. I just want to know more and more. I'm really starting to pick up little nuances about you. I can tell when you're having good days or bad days by the way you write. I am so caught up in the things you choose to describe or elaborate on. It's a never-ending Pandora's box and I really can't get enough of what your mind puts out.

*

If you don't mind my asking—what is your legal situation with funds?—I know I asked if you were happy with your lawyer. I'll do anything I can to help.

*

You know it's a full moon tonight—and I am as promised writing down my thoughts to you. I am actually quite happy just now and full of hope.

There is so much to tell you. So many more letters to write—so many descriptions to give you, explanations to make.

I've never felt about anyone the way I feel about you. I still can't quite put my finger on it. One minute I think of you as a lover that's been ripped away from me—my heart hurts so much, and I have to admit that I get jealous (even though I'm not jealous by nature—or not much). When I think of you and your past or present loves, that's when I really believe we were together in that way somewhere not that long ago.

Other times, I just think of you as the other half of me—so much like me—like my closest friend—but more than that actually—a part of me. That's a less cagey way to feel. Then I'm more or less even-keeled—it's when I think of you as a lover that I get totally confused—but I suppose that's natural. I actually like when I feel a combination of the two.

Everyone thinks my idea of a romantic relationship is so skewed anyway.

But I've always been this way—but never like it is with you—it's one thing to live with someone day after day—it's another thing to have someone move into your heart and mind.

*

I'm looking forward to our next phone tryst—but I still adore writing to you.

Lorri and Damien finally come into the 20th century.*

All my love,

Lorri

---

*   It wasn't long before we were talking on the phone, although as everything with the prison system tends to be, it was convoluted and expensive. The prison phone system is something most people don't know anything about. Most state prisons have contracts with large phone companies and the calls are always collect, and the costs are hefty. There is always a connection charge—usually several dollars, and a per-minute fee after that. A call usually lasts 15 minutes before it's cut off, then you must pay the surcharge again for another call. An out-of-state call can cost up to $25 for 15 minutes. Looking back, it's shocking to realize that we ended up paying around $200K on phone calls alone.—LD

July 1, 1996

My dearest Lorri,

    I've been thinking a lot today. About all kinds of things, but they all have something to do with you. I was thinking of how you said last night that when I saw you in person, you were afraid it would scare me. The only thing I can think of that you could mean by that is your physical appearance. Lorri, you are very beautiful, but at the same time, it wouldn't matter to me what your physical appearance was. It bothers me that you would even think that, like a tiny sliver of ice going through my heart. I love who you really are, and nothing else matters.

*

Today I was wondering, thinking, contemplating all sorts of useless information and I realized that if someone were to ask me how long I have known you, I wouldn't know if I should say "a few months" or "a few centuries." Maybe both. It's a little confusing. But I love it. I would trade it for nothing.

                Sending love forever to my dear one,

                            D.

July 1996

Hi Damien,

I was thinking about what you said—that you always knew you were going to be known—I'm sure I'm not phrasing that properly, but it's funny, I've always known something extraordinary was going to happen to me—but not like being known, or famous—something quiet and magical—behind the scenes, but very powerful. I've always felt that. I'm wondering and beginning to believe it has something to do with you. I know things like this don't come easy, and this certainly hasn't been easy—but it has been extraordinary.

I can't wait to see what's in store for us—it's sitting inside me like a small growing seed—it's quite marvelous—although sometimes it's a little uncomfortable.*

Much, much love to you,

Lorri

---

* Here's a photograph of me, taken at a Yankees game the day after Damien first called me. He'd promised to call the following day, although I'd forgotten to tell him I wouldn't be home—my upstairs neighbor listened for the phone and ran downstairs to answer and explain my absence. In this photo, with my friends Luis and Julie, I'm keeping the happiest secret inside. When I read this letter, I am astounded by how accurate it was, in some ways. Looking back over the years, and what  happened to both of us, the paths our lives would take—it was as if I were looking into a crystal ball. Even now, as our lives are unfolding in the free world, I am experiencing a sense of what my words forecasted. I'm increasingly grateful for all our patience.—LD

July 8, 1996

My dearest Damien,

I am so giddy with speaking to you! It's like a whole other world has opened up. Not that it makes you any more "real" to me—it's just another layer. I must admit it makes me less anxious—at least I can direct my feelings somewhere—whereas with letters, as wonderfully romantic and dreamy as they are—I sometimes feel like they are just flying around out there—you'll get these thoughts at some point—but with the phone—I can actually hear you breathe. I sometimes stop breathing myself just so I can listen to you.

*

I find myself almost pleased with the jealousy I was telling you I felt at times. When you were telling me about how you felt about creating a child—I was secretly thinking—that's not fair—if I was going to have a child in this life—well, it most certainly should've been with Damien!!!! Isn't that funny? But I feel perfectly at ease with those thoughts. They seem perfectly natural to me.

*

Even with as much as I have loved and love people in my life—I've never allowed anyone to take up residence in my soul, but you just seem to belong there—as a matter of fact I just welcomed you right away, like you'd been away for a while and then quietly returned.

(Well, maybe not so quietly—I think you disturbed some very heavy pieces of furniture that make up my interior!)

You, I adore you so much.

*

I haven't felt like this for anyone. Yes, I've missed people before, and I still do. But with you, I don't know, Damien, it's all-encompassing. I don't know what to do about the physical part—I mean—I can write you my thoughts and now I can hear your voice—but I don't know about this physical part. It's almost over my head. Do you understand? I mean, I can't deny that there is a sexual aspect to it—I do think about being close to you in that way—which is even more perplexing not having anything to be physically attracted to—no smell, no touch, no skin—but it's there, and I feel it—but it's unlike any physical attraction I've ever had—because it does go beyond that. I wish we could just leave our bodies and meet somewhere because I get impatient with my body—it sometimes seems so base—I know the gist of my love for you is not physical—but my body likes to feel otherwise—and I'm certainly not used to feeling these things—I want to make it stop sometimes and other times I want to feel it all the more, because it's for you and all I want to do is hold you in my arms. Do you ever feel this way? And are you utterly confused by it, or does it seem perfectly fine for you? I haven't even wanted to discuss this with you—because I think or thought it made me sound weak or unevolved and I also think it very presumptuous of me, and then there's the hesitancy even speaking of it because you have probably come to terms with such things in your life and why should I assume you would ever even think such thoughts—specifically, I mean, especially about someone you've never seen. Will you help me with this? Quite possibly, it'll pass and it's a natural state in any relationship, even one as unique as ours. And then again, maybe I'll always feel these things for you—which makes me quite giddy to think about—because you are the warmest, sweetest person I could feel this way for—and I must say for now it makes me feel very special and blessed.

*

I still love writing to you—even more, now. I'm still not quite brave enough to say some things to you, but I feel so comfortable writing to you.

Yours,

Lorri

July 9, 1996

My dearest Lorri,

   Everything is so hectic right now. I don't think I can stand it.
No one understands anything. It seems that the whole world is so
cold, so unfeeling. I'm thinking of going into "seclusion" for a
while, maybe forever. I just don't even feel like talking to anyone
anymore, it's so much trouble, it's shattering my nerves and tearing
me apart. Except for you. You're the only one I even want to talk to
or think about anymore. You're the only one who understands.
You're my hiding place from the world. You're a complete, separate
universe that I can escape to.

*

I should have seen this coming, but I was blind as usual. You're
absorbing me, but you're also giving me back pieces of myself that
I had lost for so, so long. It's so painful, but so pleasant at the same
time. I don't know what comes next, but I surrender everything to
spirit, to let it happen as it will, and I will enjoy every minute of it. I
have gotten drunk off of this entire experience; my entire being is
reeling from the bliss of it.

Sending love forever to my dearest one,

Damien

July 11, 1996

Dearest Lorri,

Do you have pierced ears? I was just curious; mine have been pierced since 5th grade.

It never occurred to me to ask you before, but what's your middle name?

What's your favorite color?

What size shoes do you wear? Mine are size 13. I have very large feet for someone my size.

I won't bother you with any more stupid questions. I'll close for now. Thinking of and missing you, sending love forever to my dear one.

D.

July 15, 1996

My dearest Lorri,

You made me so happy today that there is no way I could express it, because I read some things in your letters that said things that I wanted to say, but couldn't bring myself to say. My mind is racing so fast, my hand can't keep up.

First off, let me explain about the physical contact. I'm not "above" it as you thought, because I constantly have a thought that goes around in my head—I know how you love to sleep, and there is nothing in the world that I want to do more than be able to hold you while you sleep, to watch over you, to be able to press my lips to your head and breathe in all those beautiful, magickal things that wander through your dreams. I would love to be able to trace the features of your face with my fingers, to kiss your hands. I am not talking about lust, because this is as far from lust as you could get. I would love to be able to fall asleep with my arms around you. It's just too hard to explain; the only way I know how to express it is: "For you, I would forsake everything, I would drop everything and follow you to the ends of the earth, because you are as much a part of me as my own heart and blood, you are me."

Secondly, I have thought many, many times, "If I was to only have one child, why could it have not been with Lorri?" That child would be something that I long to be—half of you and half of me. I wouldn't have even minded the morning sickness, I would have cherished it because it would have been part of you that I would be able to express with my physical body. I've thought a lot about the way I used to hold Domini while she was pregnant, the way I would trace my hands over her stomach for hours at a time, and thought, "How much more wonderful could it have been if it would have been Lorri?" Am I making sense at all? I know I'm not, but I still know that you will understand.

I cannot possibly explain how big a part of me you have become. It's like now my entire universe is comprised of nothing but you.

Sending more love than you can imagine to my dearest one,

D.

July 15, 1996

My Dearest Damien,

My whole conception of love has changed, too. It really is all-powerful—I never had any idea—it transcends all of my "limitations"—time, distance, lifetime, physical need, jealousy, fear (the big one), commitment. None of those things matter when it comes to pure love—and I am just now learning this—from and with you. And I thought I had learned so much in this life—I thought I could live through anything—and here you are—to humble me, and to make me see how much one really can endure—and still be at peace.

I love you so much,

Lorri

July 18, 1996

My dearest,

You don't know how much I loved the questions you asked—yes, I have pierced ears—although I haven't worn earrings or any other jewelry for a long time.

*

I got my ears pierced in the fifth grade, too!!!

My middle name is Ann. I think I know yours—it's Wayne, isn't it?

My favorite color is blue—what is yours? I also like all shades of gray.

I wear a size 6 shoe—

And no—those aren't stupid questions—I love them. I always want to ask you questions like that, too.

*

I would love to go out and about with you! Damien, we could have so much fun. And yes, you must see Scott Depot and I must see West Memphis! And yes, you will eat vegetables. Yes, you will. You will. Maybe just a little broccoli—it's really good.

I've never roamed around before. Being the hermit and homebody that I am. I've always wanted to do it, too, just skulk about with no particular place to go.

Sending much love,

Lorri

postscript, 2014

So much of what I was doing at this time involved ritual, or anything I could do to make Damien feel physically close to me, and to make the letters special for Damien. I addressed every envelope with a fountain pen using sepia ink, I kissed the back of each letter so that a lipstick mark would show, I opened each of Damien's letters from the right side, and I wrote a little message underneath each stamp. The stamps themselves had to be special in some way, too—no American flags or roses.

Looking back, that we were becoming so close very quickly was something I dove headlong into. There were definitely instinctual voices telling me that pain was coming, that I should slow down and think about the decisions I was making, but I was in it, and it was full-on rush. My feelings for Damien took over my life.

Somehow, I was able to continue living my professional life and to function in the world—getting up on time, performing at my job, even working sixty-hour weeks at times, but Damien was with me always.

I was very emotional at this time. I often felt unhinged, swinging way out of control. It lasted for a year or so, but I was always capable of keeping stability at the same time. I would learn over the years how to temper my emotions, but I'll never forget the headiness of the first visits, and the extremes of falling in love with a person who I couldn't be with, and who was in such peril. I knew it then, as I know it now: It was what I was made for. Damien is who I had searched for my whole life.

Lorri

July 22, 1996

My Dearest Lorri,

How could I have been so stupid? I feel like such a loser. I forgot to tell you happy birthday.

It was a strange chain of events that led me to remember. I was sitting here listening to the radio and reading the astrology book. I was reading about my ruling planet, which is Jupiter, and a guy comes on the radio and says, "This next one, by Mozart, is called 'Jupiter.'" I immediately stopped reading, and picked up your letters, which are always lying right beside me, and while I was listening, I began to wonder why all your stamps are upside down, then I remembered . . .

"Secret messages!!!" So I began peeling the stamps off, reading about when you were 6 years old, and I was completely absorbed by it, then the next stamp I peeled off said, "Today is my birthday," and my heart just sank. I said, "How could I not have remembered?" Then I immediately ran back to the phone and tried to call you, but you're not home, so now I'm writing this letter. I feel so bad, how could I have not said something? I'm so, so sorry. I can't believe I was so stupid.

Love forever to my dearest one,

D.

July 23, 1996

My Dearest Lorri,

It's driving me insane that I won't be able to talk to you tonight. I miss you so much. I just keep thinking about how I will get to talk to you face-to-face in just 4 days. I can't believe it. I'm going to try not to cry when you leave, but I can't promise anything. ☺ I'll just be glad when this is over, and we can sit and talk for as long as we want, about anything we want, with no glass between us, and no phone that cuts off in 15 minutes. It'll be so great. But until then . . . I see you in 4 days!!!

I was also thinking about what you said about there being so much in New York that you wanted to show me, and I formed a plan. As soon as I get out of that courtroom, I'm going to the nearest phone I can find. I will call and tell you I'm free, and I'm on my way. Then I'll go straight to the bus station (I'm not flying anywhere unless I can fly with you) and off I will go. I've only ever ridden the bus once before, all the way from Oregon to Arkansas, and I thought it was pretty fun. I wonder which is farther away, New York or Oregon? It seems like Oregon would be. A long, long road trip. That sounds so wonderful after having sat here in one place for so long. When I was on the bus, I didn't even get carsick for some reason. Maybe it's because it's so much different from being in a car. Can you drive? I don't think I could force myself to do it. It's scary. Listen to how I'm rambling on. I didn't think I was nervous or excited.

I can feel everything here coming to a climax, I can feel it with every part of my being, that's why I believe so very strongly that I'll be out of here soon. And I can't wait; I'm just so excited. It may sound strange, but until you found me again, I was a little afraid of being released after being here for so long. But now, I can't wait, because I know that with you, there are so many more wonderful things in store. I would love to take you to the lake by which I used to live, and just sit quietly with you all night, watching the light reflect off the water, thinking. And I want so bad to be able to see the town where you grew up, to be able to see the very place that you were born. It would be wonderful.

Sending so much love forever to my dearest one,

D.

July 24, 1996

My Dearest Lorri,

I wish I could just explain what you mean to me, but it's impossible. I can't put it into words. I have to try, when I talk to you on the phone tonight, to explain myself, but I know I will fail miserably. Maybe if I try to write it and explain it, I can somehow make you understand at least a little.

So here goes, this is the only thing I can think of: For so long now, the quote, "In my darkest hour, grace did not shine on me" was my philosophy, my outlook on life; it became my "trademark." But now I realize that the only way I could say such a thing is because I was blind. All the time, grace was shining on me, and it was shining more brightly than a spotlight, and the only reason I couldn't see it was because it shone so brightly that I had to close my eyes to it, or it would have burned them out, as if I had been gazing directly into the sun. My eyes were closed so that I couldn't see it, but that didn't mean it wasn't there all the same. Now, it's as if my eyes have been opened, and I can actually see, and everything is so beautiful that it couldn't even begin to be described by the human tongue.

For so long, I kept asking, "Why is this happening to me? I haven't done anything to be punished like this." But once again, I was only able to say that because I was blind. Now I see that it's not a punishment, it's a reward! It's the reward of a thousand lifetimes, and now I ask myself, "What have I ever done to deserve a reward like this?" And I'm more happy than I've ever been in my life, in any life. And I'm more thankful than anyone could ever imagine. It's as if now I truly know how the saints felt when they were completely swept up in ecstasy, in bliss, and they would form the stigmata of Christ on their own hands and feet, or be able to hear the angels whispering, or even singing to them. I know how it feels. And I know that nothing else matters, because grace did shine on me and you are my grace, and I love you for it. Maybe I can explain it a little better when I talk to you tonight. Maybe you'll understand. I know you will.

Sending love forever to my dearest,

Damien

July 24, 1996

My dearest Damien,

I can't believe when you read this, we will already have seen each other. I wonder how we will feel. It's funny, writing this . . . I feel like a fortune teller—I know the future—when in fact, I don't know it at all. Maybe there'll be an earthquake while we are together, and the walls of the prison will crumble around us and we'll just walk out together, and you'll never even see this letter.

*

Please don't be upset about me saying I may scare you—I don't mean my physical appearance—I know you better than that—I *know* why you love me, I just think sometimes seeing something that you've only had in your imagination can be jarring—and I must say I use the word "scare" in my own special way—let me think of an example . . . OK—since we've spoken of them—praying mantises kind of scare me and I truly love them. Does that help?

*

We should both try to read a book together, something we both love, or that we have never read—we could read 10 pages a day or something—(because I am so slow and you would finish so quickly). Think of a book—so will I—I love doing anything that will synch us up even more—if I could breathe in the air you breathe or wear your clothes, I would. Maybe we could read *Interview with the*

Vampire, since I've never read it. What do you think? I'm going to read it, anyway.

*

I know that you will be the only one who truly understands me, Damien. This, I know. There is no doubt. You already do—and I understand you. All my life I have been so sad that no one could see me, or hear what I was saying, sometimes so quietly, sometimes screaming at the top of my lungs. But you know. You are my true one. And I'm so happy and feel that *all* the pain and struggles were worth it.

Thank you a million times.

Thank you for enduring.

*

This letter has now spanned from Tuesday night to Wednesday morning.

Sending much love to you,

L.

July 29, 1996

My Dearest Lorri,

Today is Saturday, the day after I saw you in person for the first time. I couldn't write last night, I just had to lie and think. I don't even really know what I was thinking, I was just drifting, feeling you. You are very beautiful, but still so simple at the same time. I don't even know what I mean by "simple"; it just seems as if you are so "uncomplicated." It hurt me to see the way you had chewed your fingers. I just wanted to kiss them, to kiss the places where you had chewed the skin away.

I felt extremely frantic twice. Once was when you began to cry, and the other was when you had to leave. I felt so desperate, there was nothing I could do, and it was ripping me apart. I couldn't even touch you, I couldn't do anything to make you feel better, and because of that I was in agony. It was a sense of desperation that was so close to being overpowering that for a second I thought I would lose all control. When you had to leave, I just wanted to scream, "No, no, no, no." But I knew that if I ever started, then I would never be able to stop. I could see it very clearly in my mind: I would have been sitting in the corner with my head in my hands, eyes clenched shut, mouth in the shape of a perfect "O," just screaming and screaming, but not being able to hear myself. The only thing that kept me sane was knowing that one day soon there will be no glass wall, and no one to come in and say it's time to leave, and no one on either side of us constantly making noise.

That's the only thing that kept me sane. Seeing you walk out the door was the worst pain I have ever felt. At that moment, I would rather have gone blind than to have to see you leave.

Isn't it so wonderful to be completely overpowered by these feelings and emotions, even if they do also bring pain? To feel it so strongly that it destroys any hope of rational thought, action, or feeling? I love it. It's impossible to not be completely swept away, devoured. Nothing else could even come close to it. This is what I have been looking for my entire life, but I never even knew what I was looking for. All I knew was that I had a huge hole in me, a sense of emptiness that nothing ever filled, but now I have a sense of being complete, the hole is gone, the emptiness is gone, the pain is gone, everything is gone, and now everything fits together. This is why I am here, this is what was meant to be. Words are so useless now, it's as if I could keep talking forever and still never even come close to saying what I want to say, what I feel. But I know you understand.

Yesterday, I loved when we were both silent as much or more than when we were talking. The bits of silence were when I could feel the strongest sense of peace, the feeling of all being as it should be. I wish I could have prolonged them for eternity. To be able to just sit and feel you, look at you, to know you are so near. It's just one more thing in a long list of things that I will never be able to describe.

*

Another thing I really hate about being here is that I have to wear the same clothes all the time, I can never wear what I want to. And today, I have an incredible urge to wear a suit, vest, and tie. I don't know why, it's just something I feel like doing today. I thought a lot about what you were saying about wanting me to let you dress me in your clothes, and how you think it would be fun, and I have another idea, another plan. One night, you can dress me completely as a woman, I will dress you completely as a man, even hide your hair under a hat, and we will go out like that, just to see if anyone can even notice. We have to take lots of pictures, and we have to ride in a horse and buggy. Maybe that would be great. It would be just like in *The Witching Hour* when Julian and his sister did the same thing. She was evening smoking a cigar! They became the scandal of the entire town. We have to do that.

*

I thought you were going to start crying on the phone this morning, I couldn't take it. It's unbearable to hear you cry, especially when I can't be there to help, to hold you. It's agony. You were talking about how you felt bad because you were losing control. Lorri, it's not bad if you just stop trying to control it. Just release all control and let it happen as it will, and I promise that you'll feel better, you'll love it. Just let it run and spread like wildfire. Trust me, OK? Everything's going to be fine. We're together, and nothing else matters. Just let everything else melt away. Nothing else matters.

*

They just told me that my father and his wife will be here to see me on Monday. This will be an ordeal. How will I carry on a conversation with anyone in the state that I'm in now? I can't pay attention without drifting off, I can't even think without my thoughts coming full circle to land right back on you, constantly wondering what you are thinking at every moment, wondering what you're doing, wondering exactly how you're feeling. It's a never-ending cycle. I wonder if my father will even be able to tell the difference. He always seems to be so caught up in himself that he more than likely won't even notice. I guess that's good for now though. At least I won't have to answer 10,000 questions, the main one being, "What's wrong?" I hate that question, and it seems that I hear it more and more often lately. Oh well.

Forever and after to my dearest one,

Damien

my dearest damien:

i don't even know how to begin — we had just started talking about what this means. what this all means — at this moment — i'm completely drained and exhausted and weak, i don't feel like i'm going to make it. i'm not there (or any where with you...) i don't want to be without you. i don't want to go home. i've never felt so lost and alone in my life. this can't be — how can this be? what is the reason for this torture? i feel like i'm in a daze — and i'm sorry but i can't stop crying. i can't. as i was driving away — i just couldn't believe it — how can i be leaving him? how can i just leave him there? i've been driving around on roads. i don't even know where i am — i found a state park, so i'm sitting on the ground getting completely bitten by mosquitoes. you are so very beautiful. you are more beautiful than i ever imagined you could be. you truly render me speechless. i'm suddenly very confused.

its like you said... what does it
mean? why is it happening?
i honestly thought that by seeing
you, things would be easier. Why
did i ever think that? my heart
is just hurting so much. oh - i got
the book - thank you very much - although
it was meant for you - Do you have
a copy?
i am absolutely delirious. i can't believe
i haven't told you - its my one dramatic
moment on this planet - i stopped at a
store to buy this paper - it was still near
you, near tucker. i was crying and
just couldn't stop - but i didn't even care -
there wasn't a thing i could do about it
and those tears needed to come out -
i stood up out of the car - walked
2 or 3 steps - vaguely caught the
edge of the car and passed out.
right there - its weird - i ~~fel~~ fell to
my knees - because they're kind of
skinned up - some man came and
helped me up. i just went into the
store anyway. nothing matters to me

there right now but you. i don't even want
to live without you. i can't.
Damien — whats to become of us? i'm
sorry i freaked you out with my age —
i just assumed you knew and i've
sort of put it into perspective already —
i don't quite know what or how you feel
about it — you seemed shocked.
i hope you are o.k. i don't put much
relevance into age — i never have.
Some people are kind of 'ageless' — you
being one of them. i suppose i never thought
i would be feeling this way about you,
either — so now you can understand
my confusion when it came to feeling
like i was falling in love with you.
and i am. i am completely in love with
you — you are the truest, dearest, craziest
love i have ever felt. i know how
those twins felt — because i have what
feels like a huge rip in my chest right
now. it hurts so much. i want so much
to touch you, Damien — like i've never
wanted anything else.
i must say, i never expected you to be as
breathtakingly beautiful as you are.

i found myself so happy to just sit here and stare at you. i just wanted to drink you in - no human, no — nothing in my life has ever been so beautiful to me.

i keep telling myself - all the things that make up what we are together - of course they are going to be bizarre and extreme and passionate and hurtful and euphoric and wonderful - and maddening. how can't something like this, like us not be everything in the world? every feeling.

oh, i try to just be thankful for it and live it - and be so happy that you are here in my heart with me - but i am not strong at the moment and i want you. i want you totally - i want all of you - everything hurts - every part of me wants you. i want to talk with you, i want to see you, i want to read your mind i want to laugh with you i want to bite you and i want to feel you inside me. any way you can be there - thats where i want you.

but i'll take whatever we have. i'll
take whatever crumbs are thrown
our way at this moment.
but we'll be together, Damien.
i know it.

i'll risk anything for you.

O.K. i'm going to try to drive to the
    airport, now.
i can't wait to speak with you
    tomorrow.
Please know that i'm
    thinking of you
        constantly.

with all the love in my being,

            Louis.

July 29, 1996

Dearest Damien,

I am now at the airport in St. Louis. I can't believe it—I passed
out *again*! I don't know what's going on. I feel so weak. I tried to eat
a plum (I didn't buy the peach because of what you said about
sharing it) but I couldn't eat it because I got sick. I wonder how you
are doing. I just hope you are O.K. I'm a fright to look at—I swear I
look like I've seen a ghost. Suddenly I have huge black circles under
my eyes and I am white as a sheet.

Damien Echols—what have you done to me? I *am* smiling as I
write that. This is the only thing that makes me feel better, to write
to you—have some kind of contact with you. The people in the
airport—they're all scared of me—you know, they try to make small
talk sometimes, but when they see my teary face they turn away—
don't want to look. It's funny. I don't want anyone to talk to me,
anyway.

I'm so happy that finally in my life I feel like loving someone—it's
a wonderful feeling. I always thought it would never happen to me.

I feel like I don't even *need* to eat or sleep anymore.

The woman who took me out—she was nice—I tried to explain
to them that Mr. Martin at ext. 403 had arranged for me to stay
another hour—she tried—but she couldn't find anything in
writing—she kept calling me "Lorri," [everybody called me

Ms. Davis, and sometimes Ms. Echols] and she made sure I got the book.

I suppose it's good to know we really exist—isn't it? It just made it worse for me. I kept saying to myself that your appearance didn't matter to me—but I can't say that anymore. Your arms are so lanky and beautiful—your hands I will never forget. I truly have never seen such lovely hands. And your eyes. It's true—looking at your skin—I know what it feels like—it's perfectly smooth—it has that coolness of very, very white skin.

O.K. I can do this. I can accept this day. I can live with the pain— because to not live with this pain of longing—means to not live with you—at least for now.

So I will be very, very strong.

I will make it once again a part of us, because I can no longer say a part of me—because that no longer exists.

I am happy. I now know where you are. I can see you, I can imagine the place.

I called Susan from the parking lot where I passed out and I was almost hysterical—I couldn't figure out what to do because this makes no sense to me. Susan's great—she just tells me what *I* would tell me . . . Lorri—just live it (Damien, it's what *you* would tell me— just relax). So . . . I am trying now to relax. I have never had a harder afternoon—you know, even when I knew I was leaving David and my heart was broken and I thought the pain would never go away— well, this afternoon was different. It was like I knew you were so close—I could've been breathing the same air—and I felt like I was just lying in a field—well . . . maybe because I *was*! I was so scared— but I don't know why.

I must tell you something very funny, that I realized just now. I was looking out the window of this plane and I was biting my lip and looking in a certain way and I felt like I had *your* face. I think I managed to engrave your mannerisms in my mind.

I have to stop, now.

I love you.

Lorri*

---

* How I remember this time. I'm not a fainter, yet I keep reading these references to passing out. I do remember that when I flew to Arkansas, I wasn't taking care of myself. I was doing this very emotional thing—going into a prison, seeing someone I loved who was on death row. I went about it in a very demanding way. I flew down and arrived late at night, got up very early after tossing back and forth in bed, went to a very early morning visit with Damien, then flew back to NY that very afternoon. I ate nothing, it seems, in the whole time I was traveling—too nervous. Just going into a prison is taxing. Later, when I lived in Arkansas and visitors would come, I would tell them they should spend the night before flying home. Going into the prison, seeing Damien—all of it is too exhausting, both mentally and physically. Yet I went about it this first time as if I were superhuman, and I wasn't. Far from it. I suppose I really was out of my body for much of this, but then again, I was in the most surreal time of my life. When I read of this time, I actually don't recognize myself. That's how far I had pushed past my "acceptable" boundaries. My psyche was telling me that I was completely out of control, and my body was telling me that this was something only crazy people do. I wasn't listening to either.—LD

July 31, 1996

My Dearest Lorri,

For some reason, I feel a little guilty because you said that you thought seeing me in person would have eased your pain a little, or have made things a little easier for you. But I knew that wouldn't be the case, I knew what my physical appearance would do to you, I knew how it would make you feel. But I had to see you, to sit in the same room with you, to drink you up. It also ended up being a double-edged sword, because I was entranced by you, I would be content to sit and watch you forever. You are beautiful. I don't think I've ever seen a more beautiful creature. I know I've never seen a more beautiful creature. No one and nothing has ever held my attention so completely and totally as you do. I wanted to hold my breath every time you moved.

The only reason your age "freaked me out" is because I feel so much older than you, and I guess it just slips my mind sometimes that I'm not. Your age doesn't matter to me, it just shocked me for a second that you could possibly be older than me. That's the only way I know how to explain it, because once again, "the words don't fit." I know you will understand what I mean.

You asked what's to become of us. I have no idea, but we have forever to figure it out, and I will never take even a single second of it for granted. I have always despised time, because it slips away like the wind, and I never notice until the day comes when I look back and realize all that has passed, all that has happened, and all that has changed, then I feel the cold black emptiness creeping over me again, but you make me realize that time is not always my enemy. Because with you, not even eternity would be enough time.

You were also talking about falling in love. I've been steadily falling deeper in love with you ever since you asked me about chastity belts, whirling dervishes, 17-year locusts, and Paganini. From that moment on, I was completely swept away. You are the most lovely form of poison. This is true magick, magick in its purest, rarest, most powerful form. It's everything in the world.

I know how you feel, because I want you too. To be completely lost in you, to let the world dissolve until only you're left. Just relax right now, though, we have all the time in the world and we will be together. All it will take is just a little more time. I know it's hard to have patience, so I just keep telling myself that I've waited such a long, long time for you that a little more time isn't going to be so bad. I can do it. You make everything worthwhile.

So you want to bite me that bad, huh? You can bite me all you want, but I give you advance warning—I will trade your every bite for a kiss—your hands, your face, your lips, your ears, it doesn't matter. But every time you bite me, I will kiss you.

Sending all the love I am capable of giving to my dear one,

Damien

August 1, 1996

My dearest Lorri,

I received the most beautiful letter from you today, though I
doubt you were feeling very beautiful at the time. It's the one you
wrote from the St. Louis airport. The emotion was so strong, and I
could feel it so clearly. I could see you writing it in my mind, and it's
so beautiful. It affected me so strongly, I was throwing up, couldn't
stop shaking and crying. Not to mention cramping up. I just love
you so much, and it's causing so many wonderful, painful things, in
my body, mind, heart and spirit. I could never express with words
how dear and special you are, how much you mean to me.

*

You were beautiful beyond description. I was trying to memorize
everything about you, so that I can reconstruct it in my mind again
and again. I love those little tiny lines around your eyes. And I
couldn't decide if your eyes were grey or light green. But I love
them. Everything about you seemed so tiny, but your ears were the
best. I would love to kiss them.

*

I feel so completely overcome with emotion right now that I don't
even know what to do or say anymore. So I only sit here, thinking to
myself. It's all I can do.

Lorri, next month my case goes before the Arkansas Supreme
Court. A few people are building up energy, which they will focus

and release to help the case along, but I need you, too. I need you to every day, concentrate with everything you have for a few minutes on pulling me to you. All you have to do is pull as hard as you can. I don't think you even realize just how strong you are yet. You have very powerful natural gifts. Just pull me to you.

I love you more than you can imagine, beautiful creature,

D.

August 3, 1996

My dearest Damien:

I have been crazed all day—I couldn't wait to get home so that I could write to you. The letters you wrote after you saw me were so incredible. So beautiful. I like what you said about me being "simple" and uncomplicated in my physical appearance. That is exactly the way I see myself. It's funny, too, when I talk to people who know me about their first impression of me—it's always so different from what they know. They usually think I am how I look, which I am—I think—but there's that whole other side—the "spooky" side that no one sees and that you alone know. I like it—it makes me feel like I have a natural camouflage—I can't be seen.

Whereas you—you are so uncannily physically beautiful that you draw people to you—in a way that must be exciting—is it scary sometimes? Those beautiful, full-of-everything eyes of yours—I just want to look into them forever. I will never forget them. Once again—the opposites of each other—you the male in body, but so exquisite—me the female but so straightforward—kind of like the ducks! (But the opposite.) I love it.

I would love to see you unclothed—you must be a vision— sometimes I imagine what your body would look like—very thin and delicate in a way—but so fine—like porcelain—every vertebra would show—ribs, too—very little hair, but where it is, it is very black. Lots of shadows on your body—can see blue veins through the skin in some places. White, white skin—not even stretched

across bone—it fits you perfectly—there is no strain—unmarked—
so, so beautiful. I know you are.

*

I am fortunate in the fact that I don't suffer from the American
female "I hate my body" state of mind. I have always loved it—not
the way it looks—or any vain aspect—but that it's me—it does
wonderful things for me—why not respect it? I can't understand why
people mistreat or hate their bodies. I feel sad for them . . .

Oh you . . .

You just called and I must say I have never wanted to be with
someone so badly as I want to be with you at this very moment. My
whole body is alive with it . . . it *is* agony.

*

In complete and bewildering love,

Lorri

August 5, 1996

Dearest Damien,

   You asked me today if I was surprised at how fast things have happened with us—if I even imagined after I mailed the first letter—I think I'm only relieved—that you are who you are—I honestly don't think the feeling of "surprise" has ever come about. Confusion sometimes, even a slight feeling of fear—because of the profound nature of it all—I suppose the way people who finally or first experience a true miracle or see their efforts or sincere beliefs come to pass—there can only be a small amount of fear—but that has gone, now. What about you—are you surprised? I suppose it's a little different for you—I mean, for me it was like a lightning bolt hit me, literally. I was kind of in shock for a while until I figured out what to do—but for you—I just sort of called out and you were there. Are you surprised?

Completely with all my love,

Lorri

August 7, 1996

My Dearest Lorri,

Last night, after we talked I was so upset and hurting so bad that
I was going insane. I didn't know what to do, so I called Rick.* As
soon as he answered the phone, I didn't even give him a chance to
say anything, I just began to rave like a lunatic, about pain and
beauty, life and rebirth, destiny, chance, and just about every other
abstract concept you can think of, and I was crying so hard that I'm
surprised he could even understand a word I was saying. When I
finally shut up, he sat there for a minute, completely silent, then
took a deep breath and said, "So the rock star's in love, huh?" I was
struck completely dumb! Then I started laughing! I couldn't believe I
was so transparent. I think the strangest part was that he completely
and totally understood. I knew beyond a doubt that he understood
what I was feeling, even though he couldn't feel it himself. Just like
your friend Luis, and what he told you. They both understood.
Maybe they can just feel it radiating from us or something. Maybe

---

* I met Rick when he first wrote me a letter in the midnineties. He was a dealer and
trafficker in prison art by notorious inmates, such as Charles Manson, John Wayne
Gacy, and Richard Ramirez, among others. His initial pitch to me was that he could
"find a market for my work." He and his partner used to come see me at the prison
and take my paintings and artwork to sell, though I never did see my cut of the sale
if there was one. When Lorri and I started writing to each other, he did do us the
favor of storing our letters and keeping them all in one place. (Except for, I suspect,
the few that have found their way to eBay and elsewhere.)—DE

only someone completely dead wouldn't be able to see or feel it. I don't know. It must be extremely powerful.

*

Yes, it will be so wonderful to be unclothed, completely naked with you, to have absolutely nothing between us. I would love to trace the shape of your entire body with my fingertips and mouth, to kiss every inch of you, from head to foot. To be able to have my arms around you, holding you against me, just flesh against flesh, nothing to separate us. That is the way I would want to stay for eternity, to just hold you forever.

I love you,

D.

August 8, 1996

My Dearest Damien,

Speaking to you on the phone tonight was *so* fun—I like finding out things about you, like you've acted. I would *love* to see you act—I know you would be so great at it—you have such presence. So . . . you were in the gifted program—that's so funny because I was, too (as I told you)—did they have you take an IQ test? They did me—you had to have at least a certain IQ to get into the gifted class—I liked it a lot because we got to get on a bus and go to a whole other school for 2 days out of 5. That's where I learned how to play chess and develop black-and-white film.

*

Damien—it would be *so* fun to have a bookstore together! I've been thinking about it. I can't stand it that you don't get each and every book that's ever sent to you.

I have an image of that bookstore in my mind—what a wonderful place.

*

I'm lying on my bed, in my bedroom (imagine that—a bed in a bedroom (!))—the walls in my room are very pale yellow, the floor is wood, my bed is very plain—I have one lamp (very old) and a clock that is a ½ hour fast. There is nothing on the walls except a mirror I bought on Broadway 5 years ago. I like things very, very plain—bare almost. There is one window in here with a plain white curtain. This is where I always talk to you. I want you to know where I am.

*

D: Will you try to explain your feelings of getting a second chance? What do you think it means? In a way, I think I know—even though I said I feel so new at *this*, meaning dealing with it—I feel we've been here before—I have felt that strongly since I found you. Also—could you tell me what you wrote about my breathing? I was so giddy on the phone—I wanted to hear more about everything!! Everything about you.

I love you and I miss you,

L.

August 12, 1996

Dearest loved one,

I just got off the phone with you and the thought of being in a bathtub with you is far too much to think about—*wow* I really love being attracted to you, it makes things like taking a bath or scratching your back take on a whole new meaning—do you like bubbles in the bathtub? I like just clear water—but very hot—till you almost pass out. We can lie in there together for hours and read to each other. I just love you *so* much!

How do you feel about spending the whole day in bed? That would be the best—reading to each other, eating ice cream or toast all day—sleeping for a little while—and yes—you *will* be very close to me while we sleep—making love—then starting all over again. That is my idea of a perfect day.

No one would bother us.

*

I like reading descriptions of people in your life. It's funny, I would like to meet people who are close to you—but for now, it's almost like how you described reading a book—I want to know them through you. I want to know how you feel about them—what they mean to you—why you love them, why you don't. Like, I kind of know why you love Jason—but what was it that drew you to him to begin with? It's funny isn't it? Thinking about these things. Is it a look, a feeling, a gesture, does it take several events? It's like *Franny and Zooey*—again—little things that make a huge impact. For me, it's always recognizing a fierce yet calm independence in a person. So if I have the luxury, sometimes it takes a while of just watching them—if I am in the least bit intrigued. It's funny though—I haven't been even slightly intrigued with anyone or anything since we've become *what we are*. I struggled with that—because I don't know what to call us—is there a word for it?

David called me a zombie the other day. My friends Luis and Susan ask me about once a week if I am ever coming back. Isn't it funny? I am now living in a world with you.

Yours,

Lorri

August 13, 1996

My Dearest Lorri,

It's hard to explain what I meant tonight when I was talking about losing you. I've lost everything in my life that has ever meant anything to me. It's always been snatched away from me in one way or another. But I've always managed to recover. But you and this entire experience mean more to me, are more magickal, than anything I've ever known. And if I lost you, there is no way I could ever recover. It would be like someone cutting me in half, and trying to live through it. Sometimes I just get so afraid that you will be the crowning glory of all my losses. And it scares me more than anything ever has. I don't even like to think about it.

I love you,

Damien

August 14, 1996

My dearest Damien:

   I do think we should live in some old Victorian house
somewhere—a real haunted-looking house—maybe it *should* be in
New Orleans—for some reason I've always felt drawn there—and
you would have Rick and I would have Miss Fern.
   I just had such a mixed-up happy/sad conversation with you on
the phone. Damien . . . you *have* to know that I am *completely* with
you, I will *never* leave you. You must never think about that.

*

Don't ever forget or lose sight of how we found each other. Don't
ever lose faith—it's the strongest thing we'll ever have! It is truly
precious.

                                        Bye for now,

                                            Lorri

August 14, 1996

My dearest Lorri,

   The last IQ tests I had were when I was in kindergarten. The first
time I took it, I was only half trying. About 2 weeks later, two men
dressed in suits came to the school and made me take it over again
while they watched, and I tried as hard as I could because I was
scared that I was in trouble for not trying hard enough the first time.
They finally called my parents to the school and called my teacher
and therapist in to tell everyone what was going on. They said the
reason I had to take it twice was because my score was so high
that they believed someone had to have told me what to say, but
I scored even higher the second time. After that, they would
come back to school every couple of months to talk to me and
ask me questions. I wasn't afraid of them after the first time,
because they always brought me candy when they came back. They
would always make notes when they talked to me, and now I
wonder who they were, what they were writing about me, and what
happened to all those notes. They would never tell what my score
was, but they explained that your IQ doesn't show how smart you
are—it shows how much you have the ability to learn. So technically
speaking, a person can have a very high IQ but still be an idiot if

they don't use it. They said I had an extremely high recall ability, which basically makes me a parrot. I remember 85% of everything I read or am told (but I forgot to tell you happy birthday, so I'm still an idiot).

*

Since you described your room to me, I guess I should do the same. The walls are white, and the floor is brown. I have a small mirror over the sink, but it's made of metal and it's so rusty that it barely casts a reflection. I have a white metal table bolted to the wall. Actually, you can't even see the table, because it's piled so full of books and papers of every kind. It's piled so high that stacks of stuff are constantly spilling over to land all over the floor. There is a concrete slab which is supposed to serve as a chair, but mine is piled high with even more books and paper, which is also constantly spilling onto the floor. I have a green wooden box sitting against one wall; it's about 4 feet long, 2 feet wide, and 2½ feet deep, a lot like an old trunk. This is also full of old books and papers (and serves as a house for the rats) and on top of it is piled even more books and papers. There's also a concrete slab that serves as a bed, and next to it is a cardboard box filled with all sorts of assorted garbage. That's pretty much what my room looks like—a garbage dump. I have a bad habit of hoarding things, no matter how meaningless, until it turns into one giant clutter. And even though my room is only 9 × 12 feet, it still sometimes takes me a couple of hours to find something that I may be looking for, and usually by the time I'm halfway through the search, I forget what I'm looking for because I become so entranced by all the other strange things I find that I had forgotten that I even had, like golf balls, plastic dinosaurs, Q-tips, pieces of multicolored origami paper, and much, much more.*

I love you forever,

Damien

---

* I would come to realize the magnitude these small treasures had on Damien's life after he was released. I would open the refrigerator to find bits of aluminum foil, drinking straws, plastic cups—all stored in the side compartments. There would be such a stash of these items, and I wouldn't know what to do with them. It seems they were precious commodities in prison. Foil could be used to keep your food from the rats, a plastic cup was a luxury, and a straw was a golden ticket. Damien used one straw he was fortunate enough to come across for years.

So I left them in the refrigerator and said nothing, along with the bottles and bottles of tap water he would store. He would reuse plastic milk containers, glass soda bottles, water bottles—the whole fridge would be teeming with what looked like a crow's haven.—LD

August 15, 1996

My dearest Damien,

   When I was seeing this movie—I was missing you *so* much—I
kept imagining holding hands with you, while we sat there—reading
those subtitles! I always sit in the very first row. The image on the
screen is so *there*—huge—I love sitting there. I hope you know,
dearest, that you will be seeing *so* many movies when you are with
me—I haven't been seeing them it seems for so long—but with
you—I feel like there is much to show you that I love.

*

Oh! I forgot to tell you—I *just* found out yesterday that the 17-year
locusts are out *this year*! Isn't it perfect—in the year we found each
other—I love it!

Yours (forever),

L.

August 16, 1996

My Dearest Lorri,

Yes, it would be so much fun to actually be able to take a bath
together. To just be able to lie there in the water, holding you, being
lazy. I would also love to wash your hair, and to be able to dry you
off when we got out. You would be the most spoiled person on
earth; all you would have to do is lie there, and I would completely
bathe you. No, I don't like bubble bath, because it seems as if I can't
get clean unless the water is clear. I also love the water to be boiling
hot. When I was at home, by the time I got out my skin was always
red as a lobster, but I loved it.

*

Michael is rather odd. No, he wasn't always the way he is now. Now,
no one could force him to even harm an insect. He's been through
some very dramatic experiences the past few years—which leads to
your next question—who sought out who. He sought me out. He
had been experimenting with different rituals and forms of
meditation to open himself up to a higher form of consciousness,
and he was going through a lot of things that he couldn't
understand, and when he would try to talk to people about it, they
kept telling him, "You need to go see Damien, you need to talk to
Damien." Everyone here knows about me, but very few people
know me. Most choose to stay away, because this is a very
superstitious place. Ever since I have been here, they have called me
"The Wicked Witch of West Memphis." Anyway, he came to me

and we got along very well. He has a hunger for knowledge even greater than my own. We learn from each other. Everyone else here is constantly playing games, and is only concerned with what they can gain or beat people out of, so we pretty much only ever talk to each other. Lately, he's been doing just like you said Luis and Susan were doing, asking, "Are you ever coming back?" Only he keeps asking, "Where are you at?" The only answer I know is, "Lost somewhere in the spiral." And I know that there's no way out. Once you've danced the spiral dance, you can never return.

What drew me to Jason? Because we were the only ones who could comprehend each other's pain, we were drawn together because no one else could ever understand. The first time I ever saw him, he was sitting at a table all alone eating lunch, and his eyes had a faraway look, as if he was stuck inside his own head, and he was. We both thought that everything we would ever attempt would fail and turn to dust, that we were completely doomed before we ever even began, that no one would ever understand. We both felt trapped, and we clung to each other like a life raft in an ocean of misery. We had so many plans and dreams that we knew would never come to pass. An artist and a poet.

I love you forever,

D.

August 19, 1996

Damien!

It is so amazing—that we are going through the whole lovely sequence of becoming lovers—each in our own way and together— the whole beginning—some kind of attraction—me, not really knowing how you feel—one day I read in a letter that you actually tried to catch my scent off a letter—you have no idea what effect that simple or maybe not so simple confession from you did to me— from that night on—I was lost—I had already fallen in love with you—but I've never been in love and actually wanted someone physically—you must know that—all of these feelings are *so* new to me—I honestly have never known the two things together. That's why I'm so naïve about it—oh! But it's wonderful to know that I can talk to you for hours and laugh with you or even cry with you and share our secrets—think the same thoughts—but then be able to become possibly very silent, take you into my body and into my soul and share the most incredible feeling and trust you so completely— so completely that you could completely have your way with me, and that I know I could be safe in your arms as I am in your thoughts—and to know completely without any doubt that every touch or kiss or act that you would inflict (or bestow) upon me would be so exquisitely wonderful that as with our constant search for knowledge of each other—or things that we want to know or teach or find for each other—the quest for that total physical/ spiritual fulfillment (?) will never end.

I've been living all these years and I've never experienced this! I feel like such an explorer—see, right now I can't even imagine what you are thinking—it's like, what? Is she really this silly?? I'm afraid I am. Poor Damien. You really don't know what you're in for—did you ever imagine? What a silly one. Well, I'm sorry, but I find the whole thing crazily exciting.

*

Here I am, so far into this letter and I've just received three *beautiful* letters from you—and I want to respond to them.

About the IQs—I think our intelligence is very similar—I, too, retain so much of what I see and hear, like what I explained about details and seeing movies—but I sometimes can't remember simple words to explain something—even though I know them—and sometimes I can't remember names. Strange what I *do* retain and can recall. Like I can tell you who sang just about any song that was played on the radio when I was growing up—the director of most (not recent Hollywood) films and anything else he or she did—what year it was made—who was in it, so on and so forth. But I choose to know nothing about my profession—I care not for architects, designers—I like to keep my money source and my loves separate—that's why I don't really care about my job—except that it allows me to draw. I really dislike money—but in a way I'm starting to have more respect for it— because it is my link to you right now—so I will take better care of it.

Back to intelligence (what do you mean—"it could improve my focus"—whatever could you mean?) I'm sometimes amazed at how intelligent you are—sometimes you write something and I am just blown away—I am completely sucked in by your mind. I love it—it's like a constant source of information and insight.

*

It is very funny you should think of me as a ghost—I was very taken
aback when you said that on the phone. Sometimes, I feel I am a
ghost. I always have—I've never quite felt I belong in this time—or
anytime—I've always had a problem "placing" myself—but don't feel
uncomfortable about it. Only one other person felt that way about
me—and I received a letter years after he left me (he was a very dear
friend who helped me when I was very distraught in Ohio—the one
I screamed at from my car).

He said he was always puzzled at me—couldn't get it straight, he
didn't believe I was really *alive* as he was—that I was put here or
came here from a different time—that I had "haunted" him as a
ghost would. That's why I was so insistent that you explain—I'm still
trying to figure it out and I can't find Andy to ask him—he has
disappeared. Probably forever.

*

Something I didn't mention from before—I received your certificate
from the church! What was that? Did you complete a course? Have
you spoken with this pastor or the "brother"—are they nice? Did
you learn interesting things??*

Yours forever,

Lorri

---

* This was a course Damien took with a nondenominational church, studying the
Bible, and it took about a couple of months to complete. They ended with a test, on
the Book of Matthew, say, or Revelations, and then Damien would send me his certificate of completion. As he put it, they become so fundamentally fundamental
after a while, he took to his own studies.—LD

August 20, 1996

My Dearest Lorri,

So I'll be seeing lots of movies with you, huh? Actually, I probably won't see any because I would much rather watch you while you're watching the movie. To watch your facial expressions, to feel the tension in your hand, all without you being aware of it. I would look completely absorbed in the movie, but every part of my attention would be focused on you. That would be sublime, to feel the movie through you.

*

The 17-year locusts—we have to memorize every tiny detail about this year, so that the next time they are out, we can remember, and see how much we've changed, how much we're the same.
Maybe it's a symbol—now we have 2, the yin/yang and the 17-year locust. We must remember. 1996. The next time will be in the year 2013. Isn't that amazing? Envision looking at the dark grey sky that is filled with huge swarms of the 17-year locusts. Imagine their humming, as loud as thunder. Doesn't that seem wonderful?

It's so hot in here tonight. I'm pouring sweat, even my hair is wet. And the mosquitoes are horrible. The air conditioner must be out. I didn't think anyone was capable of throwing me off track, but you have proved me wrong. ☺ Sorry, I couldn't resist. You started it, it's not my fault!!

Yours for eternity,

Damien

postscript, 2014

It's funny; there were many things we experienced together while we were apart. Movies had always been a source of inspiration to me, and so I wanted to share that part of my life with him. We could see the same TV channels, so we watched the same things at times. Movies were shown over the weekend at the prison over a closed circuit channel. Sometimes I was floored by their choices; I remember they showed *Eagle vs Shark*, although I didn't see that one. . . . Damien had definite ideas about what a good movie was: It had a monster in it. I've never been a monster movie girl, nor did I ever see blockbusters, or movies with superheroes, or films based on comic books. I was stuck-up. I'd put too much time and energy into my education to waste time on "fun" movies.

Damien got out, and the first movie we saw together was the remake of the classic 1980's horror film *Fright Night*. It was horrible. I didn't know it at the time, but he couldn't really see movies, or read books, or write. He was too exhausted, and he didn't have the concentration or whatever combination of things it takes to do such things. He wouldn't for almost a year. But in the fall I asked him to see *The Artist* with me, at the Angelika [in New York]—it was the Oscar winner for 2011. The entire time, Damien writhed and twisted in his chair as if he were the Marathon Man. I told him he would never, ever see one of "my" movies with me again, and I meant it.

Now, two and a half years into our lives in the free world together, I see movies with Damien because it's fun. We see all the new horror films; *Dark Skies, Mama,* and we see every new blockbuster that comes out, even the ones that start out with the Marvel or DC Comics logo.

He does not see my movies ever, and it's fun.

Lorri

August 24, 1996

My dearest one,

I just got home, I received your shirt today—it smelled *so*
wonderful—I was completely lost in it—Damien, you smell so—the
only thing that came to mind was cloves! How can you smell like
cloves? It's agonizing—*so, so* close to you—smelling you, I found
one of your hairs on it and almost went into a swoon . . . This is
heavenly. Thank you *so* much! This means *so* much to me. This
means *so* much!!! I had to go lie down on my bed and think of you—
sometimes I get so deep in thought of you that I start seeing these
incredible images. I can't believe I am wearing something that has
been next to your lovely skin. I will treasure it until the day I die.

*

I loved your story about the preacher and your encounter with
him . . . that kind of thing is one of the first things I noticed about
you—your self-confidence—that's the thing that David was so taken
aback from—because he has always known it in me—he was so
surprised to see it in the exact form in you.

I also loved what you said about feeling protective and maternal
about our child—and watching him grow up—you are the
dreamiest. I love you *so* much. I love that you think about these
things—kissing skinned knees and us being grandparents—it makes
me feel so much a part of something incredible. I can't wait to raise
a child with you—you will have *so* much to teach him—and me. It's
going to be very difficult not to become pregnant right away with

you—the way you make me feel about it—but I really would like a little while with just you—just the two of us—

But it's sure going to be difficult.

Especially if you keep talking to me the way you just did on the phone!

*

Being in love with you is the single most beautiful, inspiring, breathtaking, erotic thing I have ever known. It is all-encompassing. I really never knew I could feel this way about *anything*.

Yours forever,

Lorri

August 29, 1996

Dearest Damien,

It's funny what you said about *Endless Love*. Those two—everyone
in that book drove me crazy, too. Especially Jade—she was so stupid
for not seeing what he was—she just couldn't see it. People always
try to mess with things that are so strong and true—because they
can't cope with it themselves—they can't live up to the intensity or
the power of it—so they try to destroy it—and that's what I meant
about how I was feeling on Monday night—it wasn't you—it was the
thought of all the people who couldn't see me—or hurt me—or
hurt *you*—people who can't see you—even though you play with
them—and I understand that, now—but I could never see the point
in playing with them. But maybe you had nothing else to play
with—I mean—you work with what you have—I just chose a
different route—which is far too elitist—for lack of a better term.
You are more humble in a way—it puts me to shame; at least you
don't look at them as not worth your time or energy. But it still
drives me crazy and I don't even mind that it does—I *want* you
to drive me crazy—I just have to make one thing clear—I am *not*
angry with *you*—I *know* that you would never hurt me— Do you
know what I am talking about?

*

. . . Today I was thinking. The first time we are ever physically
together—I mean actually *see* each other—hug each other—as soon
as we are alone together, even before we kiss—when we are

standing up—looking into each other's eyes—I am going to make absolutely certain that I am wearing a skirt—I am going to take your hand and place it between my legs where you will feel what I am feeling every hour of every day being apart from you while you have your way with me—how I feel upon waking—it never leaves me now—you have me in a constant state of sublime suffering.

I will leave your hand there long enough so that your finger goes ever so slightly inside me—my hand on yours the whole time—my eyes locked on yours the whole time—then I will remove your hand—put it into your mouth—and then make you wait.

I am absolutely shameless, now—sometimes at work I find myself sitting with my legs apart—my head thrown back, my hands on my knees—eyes closed—all I can think of is you—I truly am losing control and I love it. You must be having a great time.

*

I want you to *know* how I am suffering—that will be how I work on you—for you to know that I am constantly waiting.

Your touch, your kiss, your tongue, your fingers, your voice—

Always on the brink of hysteria—of possibly madness—

And sometimes I will take myself as close as I can to you—but I will be screaming your name—pleading for you to save me.

I am completely entranced with you, my love,

Lorri

September 3, 1996

My dearest Lorri,

I just got off the phone with you, and once again you asked me to teach you to do what I do. Lorri, I swore that I would do anything you ever asked of me, that my only pleasure in life comes from serving you, pleasing you, making you happy, but you don't really understand what you're asking me to do, you don't know what you're getting into. You see, Lorri, any type of magick, even the smallest little thing, creates a thirst in a person, and the more you learn, the more that thirst grows, until you have to fight with it every minute of every day just to try to keep it from consuming you. Once you realize that with magick, all things are possible, you only crave more, more, more. It all comes down to one thing—power. And it is the ego that craves power. Lorri, magick for the sake of magick is *bad*, it is a curse on yourself. You are supposed to let these things develop naturally, through certain practices, like yoga or meditation—and it is good, because you are also learning when they are acceptable, and how to use them properly. You remember a long time ago when I told you I didn't practice magick anymore? That's because I realized what it was doing to me. That *it* was using *me*, I was not using it. And it slows down the progress you make, because it distracts you from the true purpose you are in this life for.

Please just think about these things, OK? I only tell you because I love you. I can *not* refuse you anything, so just be careful what you ask of me.

I will now tell you how to do this one thing, the thing you have asked me for. Don't expect instant results, because it's just like anything else—practice makes perfect. You get stronger as you go.

O.K., first spend a few minutes clearing your mind and concentrating only on your breathing, counting each breath, until you can feel yourself going into a light trance. When you find other thoughts creeping in—stop—and start all over again.

Now, feel the beauty of your body, feel the sheer perfection of it, stretch, just feel how good it feels to be enclosed in that flesh. Do anything that makes you feel sexy, anything that makes you feel the power of your own sensuality, and always think, "I am beautiful." Feel and envision the sexuality coming from every pore of your body.

Then, see me in your mind, sitting across from you, looking directly into your eyes. Feel all of that power, all that sexuality running through your body, and force it up your spine and into your eyes. Force it out through your eyes *while* you are making eye contact with me. *Feel* the power, and think, "See me, feel me, want me."

That's all there is to it. It's very simple. It will also help if you burn a red candle, because they enhance love magick. You don't have to do it *exactly* as I say, you can change anything as long as it feels "natural" to you, as long as *you* can feel it, because if you feel it, I have no choice but to feel it. Experiment with it. All magick is like a muscle that must be flexed: the more you use it, the stronger it gets—practice makes perfect. It might make it stronger if you did also put a "love spell" on me first. I want you to! You can find one in any "love magick" book. It will make it stronger, bind us together even stronger.

Different people are better at different types of magick. Some people can't use some types at all—everyone is different, that's why witches form covens—so they can get as many types of magick in one circle as possible. Some people may be healers, dreamers, clairvoyants, scryers, and many other things—my specialty, what I am, is an entrancer, a spellbinder. That's all I'm good for. Everyone has to find their strong point. Yours is plainly seen—you have POWER. You can cause changes, make things happen, and bend the material world to your will. That's why I told you to concentrate on pulling me to you, because you have the power to do it. You are *very* strong. You want to learn to do what I do—but I would gladly trade it for the kind of power that you have. You have more in your little finger than I have in my whole being.

*

In your mind is the only place I can bear to be. I could not live if I were separated from you, I love you so very much. You are everything to me, and I will spend eternity telling and trying to show you how much I love you, what you do to me. Nothing exists for me except you. I belong to you, I am yours. Forever. I will do anything and everything I can to please you, serve you, and bring you as much happiness as I can.

*

Before we got cut off last night, you mentioned the picture of Seth. Do you think he looks anything like me at all? Everyone says he does, but I can't really see it.

Lorri, this book, *Endless Love*, it hurt me. It didn't start until after I finished it and started to think about it for a while. It's like it reached somewhere deep inside me and damaged something, but I don't know what. I only know it will take a while to fix it. I don't like it at all. It's so, so cold, it has no soul. Just like *Hopscotch*. How can this be?

Today is the day my case goes before the Arkansas Supreme Court, but they could take up to 3 or 4 months to make their decision. Please, please, please let it be soon. Sometimes I am on the edge of insanity, because the longing to touch you is so overpowering, it's sometimes more than I can handle.

I love you forever,

Damien

September 4, 1996

My Dearest Damien,

I have *so* much to think about—I just got off the phone with you—you got my letter about what I was going to do to you—I don't even feel odd about telling you things like that—before—I would never have *dreamed* such things—let alone writing them or voicing them—or *doing* them. This is all because of you—you have this effect on me—and you know what you are doing. Well, I just hope you are happy with the results of my suffering. I have to fight back the only way I know how at present. So, I will continue to drive you mad. Because you are slowly driving me mad! But what a way to go.

*

It is so erotic—and I love it—I've never felt so alive and excited about how I feel—and I love the way it makes *you* feel. I *want* you to think about me. A lot.

*

I don't mind at all if you are jealous—you seem so good-natured about it—that's always the way I've wanted to be jealous—it's very sweet for you to want me all to yourself—well, you needn't worry—there is no one else on this earth that I will ever love or feel about the way I feel about you.

I adore you,

Lorri

September 4, 1996

My Dearest Lorri,

This quitting smoking is so hard. Some days, I have no problem, I never even think of them all day. But some days, like the days when I miss you so bad that I am in pain, or on the days that I am scared, I can't seem to help myself. It makes me feel so weak, and I feel so guilty. What can I do? I need help.

*

You are right—some people can't handle things so powerful, so they destroy it without even realizing that they really want to destroy it. But you and I are beyond that. We could no more destroy what we have than we could destroy each other—because in essence, that is exactly what we would be doing. We aren't capable of destroying this. So please believe me, you are more safe with me than you have ever been. I could never hurt you. Never think back on those times again. That is the past. I am your future, and you are mine. Forever. I love you.

Oh Lorri, I know I couldn't possibly be tormenting you as powerful as you are now doing to me. If it was this bad for you every day, you would have long ago lost your sanity. Put my hand between your legs and then to my mouth? Are you trying to give me heart failure? If you are, you don't have much further to go, you little demon. You better remember that it will work both ways. I can do the same. If you do that, you had better be prepared to be dragged off into a dark room for 2 or 3 days at a time. There is no way I could be tormenting you this bad. I must be in hell, it's the only explanation. You remember when you said that if you could be with me, you feared that I would be in grave danger? Well my dear, if only I were with you now— Need I say more? I have never heard, seen, or felt anything in my life that was more erotic than that paragraph. I think I could have very easily fainted—my ears were ringing, and my legs turned to rubber. Oh yes, my love, you will definitely pay for that one. You just wait. I am going to drive you to the very brink of insanity from pure desire. You just wait.

About *Endless Love*— Yes, David was the only one in that book that really felt anything, but even his emotions were so weak. I mean, if that would have been you and me, I would have been a billion times worse than him. I would have thought of nothing except tracking you down, even if I had to search every corner of this planet. I would never have even slept until I had found you. I would have allowed nothing to stand in my way. His "obsessiveness" would have been nothing compared to the extremes I would go to. When I was reading the part about how they had hidden Jade's letters from him, all I could think about were your letters—and if anyone tried to hide them from me, they would think all of hell had landed in their lap by the time I was finished. That's why the story infuriated me—because I kept picturing what I would do if it were you and me, and I just wanted to scream at him, "Weakling! Coward! Get up and fight for her!" That's why it drove me crazy.

Yes, I have thought about our child and Seth meeting one day, and it seems like such a strange, alien thought to me. I don't know why. But it's something that I have thought about more than once. I wonder what it would be like? I believe that if they passed on the street, without even ever having known each other before—I believe they would still feel something. In a way, I fear Seth. I know that the day will come when he will want answers, he will be a man, and he will have questions—so he will seek me out. And what do I say then? How will I ever explain anything to him? I don't think "oops" will be what he searched for so long to hear.

Well my beloved, I have so much more to say, but it's almost daybreak, which means they will be here to pick this up soon. I want you to know that I am thinking of you every second of the day and that I love you with every breath I take.

I belong to you forever,

Damien

September 6, 1996

My Dearest Damien,

What I was trying to say tonight is that I feel *so* fortunate that I found you in this life when I did—we have enough time to get to know each other *so* well emotionally and spiritually, and a little if not a lot physically in this very bizarre, wonderful way—and we're still able to do things I've never wanted to do with anyone else— meaning—we can live together til we are very old, we will be able to have a child and watch him grow up *together*—in a sense, build a life together.

Although—I still would've been happy to meet you at *any* time in my life—this is the best.

*

2 things I want you to think about not doing . . .

1. drinking coffee
2. reading about George Sand

. . . both of them are not good for you. I think.
You know you can always suggest things for me to do/not do—

*

I think back to the nights when you first started "working" on me, how I would lie in bed—my heart racing, my body literally burning up with thoughts of you—thinking of things I wanted you to do to me—what I wanted to do to you—trying so desperately to feel you inside me—and I remember thinking . . .

You'd better stop this—he will *never* feel this way about you.

That seems like a long, long time ago. Damien, it's been wonderful falling in love with you—every single minute of it.

I will think of you like crazy tonight.

Yours forever,

Lorri

September 6, 1996

My Dearest Lorri,

You asked me do I surround myself with people that I know will let me down, or do I allow myself to believe that nothing else really matters except that one true love that may only come once in a lifetime. Well, I don't guess I have really ever thought about it before. You amaze me, the things you think of that are so strange, yet so thought-provoking. I've never in my life known anyone who would ever even think of such a question. But my answer would have to be—neither one. I've never sought out anyone in my life, never attempted to surround myself with anyone, and I had absolutely no belief in one love that may take several lifetimes to find. I thought it was only a lie people told themselves in order to keep the loneliness inside them from driving them mad—until you found me. Now I know it's not a lie, it's not a fairy tale, that one true love does exist. It was like I sat there my whole life watching the people who passed through my life, with only one eye open—like a king who sits on his throne, half-asleep, not even really paying attention to the things that pass before him, because he knows that it's not really important, it doesn't really matter. Even relationships with people in the past that were quite deep, I now realize were really not. It was as if I was almost sleepwalking through life, just smiling and nodding to people who passed by, without really giving them much thought. And then you flew in like a hurricane, showing me that everything I had accepted as truth in this life are only illusions I had created to pacify myself. And it's strange, wonderful, and beautiful, but it's also very painful, and sometimes when I *really* stop to think about it, I feel like I'll go insane, because it's like you turned a bag of weasels loose in my head, and they all have razor-sharp teeth and claws, and they all run around destroying the walls and the illusions I created. And that's good, because every wall they eat through only brings me closer to you, but it can still be painful. You said you like it when I pin you down and say, "Why, Lorri?"—But I really have no choice but to do that, because what I first mistook for simplicity in your thoughts is really turning out to be the greatest complexity I have ever known. And I need you to help me understand. Lorri, how can you even ponder these questions without going completely mad? And once you start to think about them, how can you drive them away? And when you ask me questions like that, it only makes me love you so much more. I thought there was a limit to how much you could love someone, but you've shown me there isn't, because my love for you just keeps growing and growing, even when it seems that it's impossible for it to grow any more—it still keeps growing. Sometimes, I truly believe my heart will burst.

I love you so very much, and I am yours for eternity.

Damien

September 10, 1996

Hello my dearest:

I just got off the phone with you—talking about puberty and Faust, a likely pair. I am feeling *so* close to you—you know how we always talk of driving each other mad? Well, right now—I want to be so gentle and quiet with you.

*

I love being out of society—or as far away as I can in this city—that probably sounds so odd to you. I don't know how to describe it—it's as if I want to have our situations as similar as possible—I mean only go out when I have to—otherwise I am here—completely here for you.

I know nothing of world news, of films, of new music— actually—*you* probably know more than me! Although I *do* listen to the radio—I, too, scan it for songs that remind me of you.

I can't believe I'm going to France on Friday—I'm going to have Stuart take lots of pictures so that I may send them to you. The whole time I'm going to be wishing you were with me—you and I would have *so* much fun roaming the streets til dawn—Paris is *so* beautiful!

One day my love, we will go *everywhere* together and we will go absolutely *nowhere* together—except stay in our room, with our bed and some water to drink.

I have a personal question to ask . . .

Are you circumcised?

I don't know how you feel about that—I hope you will let me know—but I am *totally* against it. It's not fair.

I don't understand why people constantly have to fix things that don't need to be fixed.

If we have a boy—no way—I would *never* let that be done to him.

*

I'm in bed. Ready to go to sleep. Do *you* sleep in pajamas? Please answer this and other important questions posed in this letter. Let me think of more.

I can't resist the typical—at what age did you lose your virginity? Was it fun?

I was 19. In a very rickety Victorian house in Morgantown, WV. Not memorable except for the house!

*

I completely adore you. I *love* to think of you growing up. In some ways I wish we *would've* grown up together.

Oh, well . . . next time.

Yours forever and ever,

Lorri

September 12, 1996

My Dearest Lorri:

   Tonight, when we were talking about making cloaks for each
other, I already had in my mind exactly what yours would look like.
It would be floor-length, with a hood, and it must be velvet. I think
you would look beautiful in either emerald or forest green. It has to
be trimmed in gold. Well, I'll make two. You have to have one made
of red velvet, too, to go with your red velvet dress. You can make
me one, too, but since I have no idea what it will be like, or what it
will go with, I want to make one myself, like I've always wanted but
never got around to making. I want one just like Raistlin's—it must
be of the blackest velvet, with a hood, gold-trimmed and floor-
length. Just like Raistlin's. I would *always* wear the one you made, I
would wear it until it was nothing but rags, but I want the black one
to be able to hold, breathe through it, feel it against my face. But we
definitely *have* to make them for each other. That will be so
wonderful. Then we will have the cloaks, the bed—and we have to
have two glasses—goblets—that no one can drink out of except us.
It's going to be great.

*

. . . I am doing an interview tomorrow, and I am going to tell them
that I want copies, so that I can send them to you. I should have
them in about a week. Also, when Burk and Kathy come down on
Halloween, it is now cleared for them to do an official interview for
the *Rat & Mouse Gazette*. Actually, there's not going to be an

interview, it's just an excuse for them to be able to bring cameras in, so that they can get some recent pictures—and I'll send them to you. They are supposed to be really good, because the guy they are bringing to take pictures is some kind of model photographer.

O.K., after I read this one, I won't read any more about George Sand. And I won't drink any more coffee. It's making me sick anyway. I love the taste of it, but my body just can't handle it. And the more I read about George Sand, the angrier I become at her. She was so cruel. She killed Chopin, and left him to die alone, crying out for her. That's just too much to handle. I can't stand reading it, but I love the fact that his love for her never died. Maybe they're together again now. I don't know.

I love you forever,

D.

September 12, 1996

My dearest Damien:

I had a wonderful night because of you—I *loved* talking about fevers and making clothes for each other. I do feel sorry for you, though; I have an image of what the clothes I would make for you would look like. I can imagine getting the pattern for a shirt mixed up with the first-floor plan of a house—I would be sewing a house!!—building a pair of pants!!

Oh, I don't want to be away from you this weekend! Damien. What a spoiled brat I am—able to go to Paris and I am *complaining* about it!! But I'm complaining because any day I can't hear your voice is torture.

I have to go back to the letter about my question to you—about who you surround yourself with . . . and *you* said you had created illusions in your life to pacify yourself—well, I don't think you created illusions—I think your life and what you believed were very much reality—like you said—you sat there like a king with one eye open, watching people pass by in your life (by the way—I *loved* your description of that)—you don't or shouldn't take notice until something *does* knock you flat so to speak—I think it's wonderful— at least you *know* when it happens! Most people don't even *know* it. That's what I mean about us being so fortunate—we both just kept taking the next step—and the way was already completely paved for us . . . we just had to take steps.

And I must say—my thoughts really are pretty simple or at least I think so—and I suppose it doesn't make me mad to think of these things—because it is almost innate in me—I've always thought this way—since I can remember—and it has if anything helped me *maintain* my sanity—to know there was something else, waiting for me—*you*—and eventually I would find it.

And when you write letters like that it makes me love you more—everything you do makes me love you more.

*

Is there any chance you will have contact visits by November? Just checking.

I love you. Terribly.

Lorri

September 17, 1996

My Dearest Lorri,

You remember the guy I was telling you about today, Michael, the one who pointed at me and said, "You're dying"? Well, he's a lot stronger than I even let on. It's not possible for me to impress on you what he is like, unless you have been around him yourself. It's like he does and says everything backward or opposite. Like when he told me I was dying, within a few hours my fever was gone, and I began to get better. It's as if his body is comprised entirely of doorknobs and kite string. I've only ever really talked to him once, but ever since I've been here, he's always called me "The Wicked Witch of West Memphis." He was giving me some lecture about how I was only using ⅓ of myself. And he's always laughing and waving those bony arms and knobby hands above his head as if he's dancing to a drumbeat that only he can hear. If voodoo were embodied in a person, he would be that person. He reeks of the deepest part of Africa, and no white man could take that out of him. His execution date is very near; he only has a few more months left at the most. I get the feeling that he could save himself if he wanted to, but he doesn't want to. And when I look at him, I know beyond a doubt that even in death, under 6 feet of earth, his body will still be doing that same jingling, jangling dance, becoming one with death, to dance forever. Anyway, for the past couple of weeks I've felt drawn to him, as if there is something he wants to tell me or ask me or something. I don't know. Why does all this strange stuff have to happen to me? It must be nice to be "normal." I have to say, this guy makes me very nervous and I don't like being around him at all. If Luis thinks I'm a "loud weetch" then he would have to cover his ears if he ever saw this guy.

*

You were 19 when you lost your virginity? I believe I was 14, or somewhere in that area. It was horrible, a nightmare. Plus, I had about a gallon of adrenaline running through me, so I was sore and stiff for a week, as if I had run a marathon. It's funny now that I can think back on it, but at the time there wasn't anything funny about it. It was a nightmare.

Yours for eternity,

D.

October 1, 1996

My dearest Damien:

Talking about being jealous tonight—and I said something like it's not in my nature to feel this way—well—that's absolutely untrue—it must very much so be in my nature—because I feel it *so* strongly with you—I really feel I must stop myself and remember what you say—that you are mine—that I never have to worry about anyone taking you away or anyone coming between us. But sometimes I become overwhelmed by these thoughts—I can't bear the thought of you being with anyone else—*I know* what you tell me and I have complete faith in you—but it's a maddening thought—and I know your effect on people.

*

It's funny, I just never thought of you being jealous about anything that had to do with me. Sometimes I would feel weak and think—he's *so* well-adjusted about this—I *know* I need to calm down about it—and maybe I will. But I know I will always be protective. By the way, it makes me feel ecstatic that you are jealous—it makes me want you *so* badly.

When you were explaining the loss of your virginity—I nearly cried—I wanted it to be *me*—I would have *loved* your adrenaline—I know you said it was horrible—but . . . I would've loved it.

*

Sometimes I do believe you say things just to hear my response—because I know you don't believe that I or any of the people (many) that believe in you are going to let you die. Secondly, even though we are in the age of proof, of science—you also know things are still at work—forces and beliefs and magick and unseen but oh-so-strange things—how can you say something like what you said? When I know you don't believe it, Damien.

I love you so very much,

Lorri

October 2, 1996

My Dearest Lorri,

I just want to tell you once more how much I love it that you are jealous. I love it so much. I guess that sounds a little strange, doesn't it? But I can't help it, because it lets me know that you feel so strongly that I am yours, that I do belong to you, and that you are not willing to lose even the smallest bit of my attention. It feels as if this jealousy is something that I need from you, and it makes me very, very happy that you feel that way. And there's nothing weak about it at all. I don't believe that. Not at all. But it's another one of those things that are double-edged, because I feel it too. Like when you tell me old stories or when I even think of some guy trying to get your attention, the first impulse that comes to me is of wanting to mangle him. And I don't feel weak about it at all. I think it's pleasant.

Good night beautiful one,

Damien

October 3, 1996

Dearest Damien,

For as many ways as we are alike—we are different—and I love it. Talking to you on the phone tonight was hilarious—when I asked you about "Matilda"—what a reaction!! My goodness. Well, we're going to have to come to some understanding. The way I look at it—if I have to carry the little thing around for nine months, practically killing myself giving birth to it—then I should be allowed to name it just about anything I want. Now, what do you have to say about that?

Well . . . OK. I'm still open to negotiations. I'm sure we'll come up with something.

*

We must never try to make one another jealous—not all the time, anyway—because I think that is cruel—some things you just can't help—like if you are telling a story—like the Italian woman, or me telling you about Neil—but this is a crazy, reckless, all-consuming emotion—jealousy—I can see why it goes hand in hand with love—sometimes. But it is also very important that we keep in mind that we needn't be jealous. Damien, you have no reason ever to be.

*

I want to know how you feel about this—every aspect of it—being jealous or knowing I am jealous—making me jealous, me making you jealous.

*

How can someone (me) endure all of these emotions? It's wonderfully crazy—and I haven't even gotten to touch you yet, for God's sake!! What will I be like after that? The mind reels.

Yours forever,

Lorri

October 3, 1996

My Dearest Lorri,

   You must be out of your mind because there is no way I would
ever consent to naming our daughter "Matilda." That's a horrid,
horrid name and no one should be forced to go through life with a
name like that. What's wrong with the name Raven? Or
Shadowweaver? Or Arianna? Or for a boy, how about Natas or
Granimer? I can see now that we will have many long discussions
over this, but never, ever will I consent to "Matilda." That's awful.

                                    *

What do I think about when I think of you and me being together? I
guess it's mostly abstract, very few solid images, but I want to make
love to you in every way that is humanly (or even inhumanly)
possible. I want to breathe your breath, taste every part of you. And
I think a lot of the way you breathe, wondering how it would be.
Sometimes I wonder about things like if you keep your eyes open or
closed (especially when you kiss, because I cannot kiss with my eyes
closed). Sometimes I wonder about your limits and expectations—
like if there are things you would not do, or what things you like
more than others. And I love the idea that I have forever to have all
my questions answered. Sometimes learning can be fun. ☺

                                                            D.

October 4, 1996

My dearest Damien,

   The sweetest thing happened today—I was working, working—
and I didn't want to stop—and Julie was going out and she asked if I
wanted anything. And I asked her to mail a letter to you—she said,
"Sure." Well, as you know I kiss every letter that I ever send to you,
and I had pre-kissed this letter. Later that day—Julie said, "Lorri, I
hope you don't mind, but I kissed Damien's letter before I mailed it.
I always see you kiss them and I was afraid this one was going
unkissed." So you'll get a kiss from me—and a kiss from Julie—
which is fine—cause—it's Julie!

Yours forever,

Lorri

October 7, 1996

My dearest Damien:

I am in such a euphoric state. I have so much to tell you—I feel so close to you and more and more in love with you each minute. Last night—when you told me about Howie's firm taking over the case—I thought I would scream—I did when I got off the phone. Damien—this is incredible—you will undoubtedly soon be in my arms—I can't help but be amazed at how everything is falling into place. Miracles happen every single day since you've been in my life—and I won't for a minute take any of it for granted.

*

Now—I must comment on the Grand Guignol and Morpheus. The Grand Guignol is very intriguing to me—Damien—you never explained how you know all of this—you know so much—have you met him? How could you know this? Who is Gracie? If you choose to go with the Grand G and he gives you a part of himself and you give him a part of yourself—where will you end up? Or is there no end? Can you ever go back or do you become something else (I suppose that is inevitable) and can you have some kind of peace with him? I like that he is playful, somewhat.

But Morpheus . . . see, I love sleep so much—but I've never thought of it as kin to death—to me it is the most "alive" thing—I look forward to it every day. However—not so much now—I just look forward to you. Sleep has just become something in the background for me. So Morpheus doesn't seem at all ominous to me. Kind of like an old friend.

Thank you for telling me about them. I would like to meet that Grand G—I would have fun with him. He sounds like he probably hangs out in a few places around here.

*

. . . I want you to be completely addicted to me—I want to be the very essence that feeds your veins—I want you not to be able to get through a day without being inside me, tasting me . . . Damien—I want you to hold me down with all your might—I want your arms—your hands on my arms pinning me down [. . .] I think of that all the time—I can't imagine a more remarkable thing. I want to be completely held down by your body—your mouth, your hands, your legs—and looking right into your eyes. I want to be engulfed by you. Will you do this to me, please?

As far as limits—there are none with you. There will be absolutely none—as I have said—you may do anything you want to me and with me—what an exquisite state to be in—you would think it to be impossible—but it's not—and I am living proof.

I, too, kiss with my eyes open.

And I *love* to kiss.

I love you more than you ever thought possible,

Lorri

October 11, 1996

My dearest:

I am always in trouble or distress or emotional upheaval when you see this piece of paper. And today, I am in all of these.

Every now and then I think of our recent conversation and I get the feeling—the same feeling as jumping out of a plane—that's as close as I can get to describing the feeling.

I am rendered breathless and limp and at the same time strangely vibrant with all of the adrenaline that is running through me, and my heart is beating so hard and my breath is staggered. You said we've been together over six months—never, Damien, has a lover had so much effect over his love—never—I am drugged with you. I want more—your words—I feel like an addict waiting for her next fix. Damien . . . and you haven't even touched me yet.

I wonder at this moment how you are feeling.

I won't be able to speak with you this evening and it is tearing me apart.

I love you so much—I adore you and I long for you as no one has ever felt such longing and I do want to be buried with you and I do want to die with you—because it can be no other way.

L.

October 18, 1996

My dearest Lorri,

No, I wouldn't say it feels as if you've invaded my realm, because I don't think my realm exists anymore. You came along and blew my former realm to pieces, forcing me to create an entirely new one.

Before you came along, I had spent months thinking about how no one was worth the effort of even acknowledging their existence, because no one and nothing brought me peace of mind or any consolation, so I was thinking about how I would spend eternity alone, and then—you came along, once again proving me to be a perfect idiot.

*

The reason I like *Nona*, the reason I've read it so many times, is because I believe it's the most beautiful love story ever put on paper. Not even Romeo and Juliet can compare. I think it's absolutely beautiful and heartbreaking. And it ends the way a love story should—he forsakes everything, even his own life, to go and be with Nona. It's beautiful.

*

You said I was a "glaring knock-down-every-roadblock Mack truck" who chose superhighways. I don't think that's entirely true, because I never chose superhighways. I made my own and they were paved with misery, sorrow, and suffering. But I had to do it, because it was my way of laughing in all their faces. I loved the feel of the human masses converging on me to crush me, only to see me break through in the end, still laughing at them. That's how I get myself into messes like this. It takes a tremendous amount for me to do it, because I had to burn as bright as the sun. And I have to admit that this time I almost bit off more than I could chew, because I was getting too old and tired to burn that bright anymore. I just didn't have the will or reason to do it anymore, so I sat here waiting for the final blow to fall. And then you came along, giving me back my youth, my will, my strength, until now I can burn again. But this time, I've learned my lesson. I don't want to tease the lions anymore. All I want is you.

And I love you. And I belong to you. And I am incredibly happy.

Damien

October 21, 1996

My dearest Lorri,

Ever since last night, when we were listening to each other, making ourselves come, I've felt that we are now in an entirely different realm, as if we have walked through a door and left everything else behind us. It feels like we've started another part of this journey we are on. It feels as if everything changed during the course of that one conversation. And I love it. I feel so much more peaceful now, almost languid. It's exquisite.

I am yours forever,

Damien

October 30, 1996

My dearest Damien:

It's strange what I was explaining to you about being
possessive . . . it's not that I think you are not mine—or that I have
to worry about you, or our love—it's like I don't think anyone or
anything has the right to have any part of you—that's why I have
such a problem with the media—I can't stand it—that is why I
stopped taking in pop culture. I don't think any of that stuff is
worthy of you or me or us—it degrades us. Like you were talking
about how the world has no place for you—I feel the world has no
place for us.

*

This morning I woke up only to have your name on my lips—not
even out of sleep and your hands were all over me and your mouth
was all over me—it was so wonderful—I can't help myself—every
time I come, I have to say your name—it just starts coming out of
my mouth—almost breathlessly—it's like you can hear me.

I love having myself surrounded with things that you used to
have—your books, your clothes—I wear the hair tie you sent me
every night to bed—but I won't wear it out on the street—nor your
clothes, yet. However, I would like to venture out in your clothes.
They would make me feel so safe.

I love you,

Lorri

November 1, 1996

My Dearest Lorri,

   I don't know what I am. If there is a name for what I am, then I don't know it. But I know that no two people see me exactly the same. Sometimes they see what they want to see, sometimes they see what I want them to see, and sometimes they see something else entirely. But if you want a name, I don't know one.

   I hate when people come sniffing around things they can't understand, things that don't concern them. Lorri, please be wary of things like that. Sometimes when people do things they believe is to help us, they can cause more trouble than they even imagine. "The road to hell is paved with good intentions." Just be careful, please.

*

I love the thought of you eventually wearing my clothes out on the streets. I think of you running around in New York, wearing a prison uniform shirt, and I can't keep from smiling.

I am yours forever,

Damien

November 5, 1996

My dearest Damien:

   No. You will not be in there for five years—absolutely not—not
with all of the power out here pulling for you. Damien, that's just
not a possibility. I feel so much lighter—shedding such a heavy
burden as fear—I hate to admit it, but it is one of my weaknesses,
and I have fought it my whole life—but you . . . I will not let fear
touch us. Not ever again—we can handle anything that comes
our way.

I am yours forever,

L.

November 6, 1996

My Dearest Lorri,

My love, I don't want you to always try to be strong for me.
Sometimes, I can be strong enough for the both of us. From now
on I want you to always tell me these things that prey upon your
mind. I want to know when you cry. And I will do anything I can
to ease the pain, to ease any fear. Just tell me.

I know that us not being able to be together right now is painful,
it hurts like hell, but all you have to remember is that we will be
together, just think about that and look ahead to the time when we
will be together constantly, when nothing will ever come between or
separate us again. We will spend every minute of every day together,
and we will leave everything and everyone behind us. It will be
only you and me. Then you will look back at this time that we
have been separated and you will say that it was worth every minute
of it. Lorri, everything is perfect, it's all just threads woven
together to form the picture. I love you, and everything will be
perfect soon.

Yes, I've only been in love once. Only with you. People can only
say they don't believe in love, or that love doesn't last, because they
have never experienced true love. If they ever felt the things I do, the
way I do, they would realize and understand that they have never
before felt true love.

You, always the victor? Yeah, and then you woke up.

How far back do I remember? I have partial memories all the way back to when I was still small enough to take a bath in the kitchen sink.

My first day of school was a nightmare. I remember sitting across the table from this black boy named Patrick, and we just sat there staring at each other all day. I had a teacher that really, really hated boys, so she was very mean to us. She used to paddle me almost every day. I remember the very first day, at snack time, my grandmother had sent me some cookies, and I wouldn't eat them because I was so homesick that I just kept thinking, "My grandmother touched these cookies." And I hated "nap time." I would always crawl around on my hands and knees, tormenting everyone who was trying to sleep, and I always got paddled for it, because someone would always tell on me when the teacher came back.

What things did I think about? I couldn't stop wondering why I was so different from everyone else. From a very early age, I knew I didn't fit in, I knew I didn't "belong," and I used to sit outside by a thornbush, on the verge of tears, thinking, "I've got to get out of here, to go back where I came from." But I had no idea from where it was that I had come.

I belong to you, only you, for eternity,

Damien

November 7, 1996

Damien,

No.

That's not it at all—yesterday when you said you could be strong enough for the both of us—and I said I was so affected by the thought of not having you—well—I suppose it has a little to do with it—but it's not the whole story, Damien, I can't bear it that you can't go out prowling late at night or that you can't eat broccoli even if you wanted to, when you wanted to.

Don't you know—I'm not crying for myself? Every tear is for you—but that's what I mean about being strong. I must overcome this weakness—I can't stand myself sometimes. I can't stand being weak—but you, my beautiful one, have managed to bring out every single solitary feeling that exists in me—so I suppose sometimes my heart will just break in two and I will just have to let it happen. I do think there is quite a bit of power sometimes in tears—I know there is in mine—it depends on how they are wept—what state my heart and soul is in.

My nights continue to be strangely magical with thoughts of you. I wake up hearing things in my head—the last two nights have been incredible—the strongest point came at 4:00 a.m.—I was lying on my stomach with my hands underneath me—

Suddenly I heard your voice so clearly in my ear and I was so startled by what I heard, it was that wonderful, low kind of "gravelly," as you call it, voice of yours and I've never heard you say something like this—but I loved it and I was strangely thrilled by it—Your voice said, "Lorri, I want to fuck you." My eyes flew wide open and a complete shiver went through me—I lost my breath and my heart was beating so hard—it was extraordinary. And if you ever say that to me in my presence—you had better mean what you say. I wonder why I was so affected by a word—or by your words—completely lovely to me, nothing else.

I have to work.

I love you.

L.

November 7, 1996

My dearest Damien,

My fever for you is getting stronger and stronger. I miss talking to
you about all the things we can do to each other.

I don't quite know what to do about that—I am going to talk to
you about it tomorrow.

When I was thinking about seeing you, I realized that you will
finally be able to catch my scent—I don't care if there is 3″ of glass
between us—you will be able to—and I will finally be able to look
into those beautiful eyes and look at those beautiful hands and
wonder what it will be like to kiss that exquisite mouth.

*

Oh, Damien . . .

I am so in love with you.

If only someone at that prison had a heart they would let us
spend even one hour together.

*

Now, we have a much more important matter to discuss: body hair.

What do you think? If women were supposed to be hairless,
don't you think they would be? What I'm trying to prepare you for
is, in the winter I never shave—I have hair on my legs and under my
arms—and I love it. That's why I was asking. I wanted to get your
honest opinion. Oh, I suppose you would come back with all men
should have beards. Well, OK, fair enough—but a man isn't

considered repugnant if he has a beard—whereas a woman's body hair is considered disgusting by our society. And why? I like cultures that revere mustaches on women—I think if women in our culture were not so concerned with being "perfect" (which, by the way, I think is perfectly scary) their sex drives would be a lot stronger.

I never understood these things.

I remain always yours,

Lorri

November 14, 1996

My Dearest Lorri,

No, my love, I don't want you to "suffer quietly" or be some sort of pure little thing. I want you to be just as you are—a raging furnace. I was only joking with you. Don't you think I love to know how much you want and need me? Don't you know that I love that you tell me of these incredible feelings that I provoke in you? I love it, and I do not want you to change anything.

*

My beautiful one, I don't care if you never shave your legs or under your arms. It makes no difference to me if you look like the wolf man, or if you're as bald as an egg. What society says or thinks a man or woman should or should not look or act like holds no concern for me. The longest I've ever gone without shaving is about a month. I can't stand to have all that hair on my face. I think it's absolutely disgusting. Plus, it makes me look like a pale, skinny Jesus.

I will never be past wanting to be physical with you. How could I be? When you love someone, it's only natural to want to be joined with them, to be one. If it were up to me, we would spend the rest of our lives in bed together. Sometimes, it's just so frustrating, because I lie here thinking about it, talking to you about it, and the longing gets worse by the minute, and I still can't even touch you. It's enough to drive me insane sometimes.

I love you forever,

Damien

November 21, 1996

My dearest love,

I was completely serious about working at Dairy Queen.

I wish I could work some place where I got paid to just look things up in books—like what exactly is a "batter's cage"?

Or . . .

How do you catch trench mouth?

I would love that. Just to have people call me and ask me questions.

I believe the job I have now requires far too much responsibility and I don't like it. No one is going to care if I tell them the wrong answer for the origins of ballet, but it will be a big deal if a large stone wall comes and falls on someone.

Well—to them, anyway.

Or maybe I could be a projectionist in a movie theater.

Maybe painting walls or polishing marble to a high sheen—that's it! A glassmaker—no . . . ego involved.

All I want to do is be with you.

How will we survive?

We'll figure it out.

I can't imagine you a marine. You are far too stubborn (yes, you are) and if I may be so bold as to say, you can be arrogant.

I don't think that's the recipe for a marine. Or any military person. I could never understand stripping someone of their identity—but that's what soldiers are, right? They are soldiers first and "people" second.

Yours,

Lorri

November 29, 1996

My Dearest Lorri,

After you left today, the rest of the day has seemed like it has taken an eternity to pass. Everything seems so different now that you're gone. Everything seems a little more cold, a little more empty, and I have to wrap myself in my thoughts and feelings for you to keep myself sane. Every time I close my eyes all I can see is your beautiful face, your tiny little ears, your legs. I love you so very much. It's driving me insane to not have you near me.

*

Yes, I will always call you my wife. It just felt so natural to say that, it just rolled out of my mouth without me even formulating or thinking of it. We are married on a far deeper level than any church could ever invoke.

> I love you more than you can imagine,
>
> Damien

December 6, 1996

My Dearest Lorri,

No, when I filed the lawsuits against the prison, I did not really
do it for any specific reason. I did it a long time ago; they are just
now coming up. Anyway, I have no intention of following them
through. I will just allow them to be dismissed. None of that stuff
means anything to me or even matters. Only you matter, and I don't
want anything to do with anything of this world. It's all a waste of
time. You are all that matters to me.

No, my love, when I come it's not your voice I hear. It's that
small sharp intake of breath you always do that I hear. And then
everything explodes into oblivion for a fraction of a second that
seems like eternity and then during that second, I completely lose
myself, there is only you, my consciousness just floating in an empty
universe comprised only of you. And then I come back to myself.
Does that make sense? I just can't put it into words. I only know
what it is, how it feels. And I love it.

I once asked my mom the same question, why she fell in love
with my father. She said it was because she felt sorry for him. She
said she felt sorry for him because he was constantly in pursuit of
her, trying to get her to go out with him, and she had told him "No"
about a hundred times, but he still kept trying. Then one day she
said he told her if she would just go out with him once, if she didn't
like him, he would never bother her again. So she said "Yes." A few
months later, they ran away to New Mexico together and got

married. By the time anyone found out, it was already done. Then, about a year later, I was born. My mother said that when I was born, I was so ugly that my father cried. When she told me that, it hurt my feelings at first, then I thought it was hilarious. She said when she first met my father, she didn't like him because he "thought he was big and bad, riding his motorcycle and smoking his Marlboro cigarettes." I thought it was funny. She also said it was hell trying to ride a motorcycle all the way from Tennessee to New Mexico and back.

I thought it was kind of romantic.

I love you so, so much. Sometimes I think we're both insane. And it's great.

D.

December 23, 1996

My dearest Lorri,

Well, tomorrow we should hear a decision from the Arkansas
Supreme Court. I don't expect anything out of them, they will do
nothing to help us, but we must pass through them in order to get
to the federal court. The federal court is the one who will help us.
Even though I know the Arkansas Supreme Court will do nothing
for me, I still can't help but hope, even though I know I will be let
down. It's still impossible for me not to keep my fingers crossed.

I do have some good news though. There is a show on NBC
called *Dateline* and they usually do a show that deals with 4 different
topics, and they spend 15 minutes on each. Now they want to do a
show where the entire hour will be about nothing but my case. This
is major, because this show is watched by the world! This is going to
be a bigger help than you can imagine.

*

p.s. I thought about it, and I think Indigo is a good name. It's much,
much better than Matilda. So Indigo it is. And it's an appropriate
name for either a boy or a girl.

My heart and soul belong to you, my loved one,

Damien

December 26, 1996

My Dearest Lorri,

Well, so far 2 out of 4 of my predictions have come to pass, but I was wrong about 1 of them, and we have to wait to see if the fourth will be as I said. I said the Arkansas Supreme Court would make a decision before New Year's Day, and they did. They made it today. Second, I said they would deny me. They did. Third, I said they would overturn Jason's conviction, and this is the one I missed, because they denied him, too. My fourth prediction was that I will be released sometime when I am 23. This is the one we have to wait a little longer to see. I still can't believe that I missed one! Oh well, practice makes perfect.

*

This is our first Christmas together. It's amazing how different everything is with you. I love sitting here thinking of the first Christmas you, I, and our child will spend together, no one but us. Isn't it incredible to even think of it? Like a miracle. And of course, the child's name will be Indigo.

I talked to the new lawyers, and I do not like them. I'll talk to you about it, but they are soul-suckers.

I feel scared now, because there is no magick anywhere when you are gone. I miss you so bad.

I love you forever,

Damien

January 9, 1997

My dearest,

I just got to work and the radio was on. It was people talking
from the Arkansas Department of Correction about the executions
tonight. Maybe it was because I hear so little in the news these
days—but I sat down and put my ear right next to the speaker and
listened to it all. They talked about Paul and his spiritual advisor was
speaking. Then they talked about Frankie. I felt so strangely
touched—like I wanted to cry. Yet, I just wanted to hold you—that's
all I wanted. After that I left work and went for a walk. Then I
became overcome by the feeling that once again—we are going to
be together, that you are going to be OK, and that everything will
work out fine—not just "fine"—the way it should be—which is
tremendous.

I love you,

Lorri

January 9, 1997

My dearest Damien:

It's Wednesday night and I just had dinner with Susan and Luis. It
was cauliflower and spinach. I may give you a grocery list
someday—isn't that a lovely thought? "Damien . . . will you please
go to the store for me?" and the list would have things like—
Parmesan cheese (grated), broccoli, ice cream, cookies, milk, potato
chips, eggs, tampons. Yes, I would sneak that in whether I needed
them or not, just to make you buy them. I can't wait to do little
things like that.

"Damien, will you stand on my back, please?"

"Damien, will you hand me my towel?"

"Damien, will you wake me up when you wake up?"

All these things are so simple. I can't wait.

"Damien, will you come kiss me til I'm dizzy?"

Sweetness.

But I was thinking today, this will be the first time in my life I will
ever employ my feminine wiles! I'm going to get you to do all kinds
of things! This will be fun! But I promise you will be duly
compensated for all of them.

Those are the things I love to think about sometimes. Sitting in a
room with you, reading a book, with your head in my lap, you
reading too, and stroking your hair. I could stay like that for a long,
long time.

We could have toast with jam and butter for breakfast. Or I could make you anything you wanted. Do you like French toast?

I would always do anything you wanted. We will be very, very happy, my loved one.

I kind of don't want a TV. What do you think? I would like to do without a telephone. But I suppose we should have one.

Imagine how differently we will view the telephone then? No longer the lifeline it is to me now. We will never have to be parted.

Yours forever,

Lorri

January 13, 1997

My love,

For the past few days, I have been lying here thinking, and I don't feel so very young anymore. Actually, I feel pretty damned old. This feeling comes upon me from time to time, but I don't believe it's ever gone this deep before. I mean, I know I'm old, but I don't always feel that way, just every once in a while. And when I feel it, I can't stop looking in the mirror, because during these times I can always see myself age a little more. I don't mean this physical body, I mean when I look at the eyes and allow myself to look as deep into them as I can, I always see my true self getting older and older. Sometimes it makes me a little happy, because I know that with age comes wisdom, and I have been collecting wisdom for a long, long time. But at other times, it doesn't make me so happy, because I will feel like a very tired, old little creature who is well past its prime. And I feel that in all this time I have spent, I should now at least be able to rest, to just lie with you forever, to touch you, to tell you how much I love you. I don't think that's too much to ask. I will be content just to be able to be near you for eternity. That's the only thing I want. To hell with anything and everything. I have not the time, patience, or mind for it. Nothing else even concerns me, just being with you.

        I love you forever, and I belong completely to you for

                                eternity,

                                Damien

January 22, 1997

My Dearest Damien,

I am so tired tonight—the full moon is in just two days and I will
put the water out. Today, I thought of us with our moonade stand
out in the middle of nowhere—just ghosts stopping by to buy our
drinks.*

I think about us being somewhere—just the two of us all the
time, too. How we will fill the day eating toast with jam. Me
drinking coffee—not you, though, you can have tea—chamomile
tea! I'll make everything for you. We'll know the woods and the
fields so well. We'll find a place to swim, and in the winter we'll go
for long walks in the snow in the cold. We'll come back to our
house and I will make the sweetest love to you that you have ever
known. Then I will read to you or we can watch some old
wonderful movie.

There is so much to do.

I had the oddest discussion with Luis tonight.

I said, "Do you think I am insane?"

And he said, "Oh yes"—but lightly and in a sweet way.

He then said, "Don't you know that is why I am here—to keep
you from flying off the earth? I will keep the points of the eyes (?!)

---

*   As Damien has explained elsewhere, he and I made "moonwater," out of water
we set out on the full moon and then drank at the same time every month. It was
another way of being together while apart, knowing what the other was doing and
that we were connecting.—LD

until you do what you have to do. You are too emotional for this world."

He knows why he is with me. It makes me feel safe in a way—like the plan is going about as designed.

I love you,

Lorri

January 29, 1997

My love,

I loved the way you described us being by ourselves with just the woods and fields and each other. I keep reading it over and over; it makes me feel so close to you. We'll spend an eternity doing nothing except studying each other, making love to each other. There is nothing else worth doing.

I like what Luis said about you being slightly insane, and him being there to keep you from flying away. But one day, you will fly away. You'll fly away with me. And I think that if both of us weren't just a little insane, we would never make it. I've always treated insanity in a joking way, but I think madness is so romantic. And I love the idea of us gradually going mad together. It seems so beautiful.

*

No more Sandman, no more Grand G. I will never go far away from you. I will always be right with you, so you should never have any fear of it being otherwise. I could not live if I were away from you. There would be no reason to even try. I am all yours, I completely belong to you, and you must never doubt it even for a second.

I love you for eternity and belong only to you,

Damien

February 3, 1997

My dearest,

    I fear I am so reckless sometimes—you are so much wiser about things sometimes. I lack discretion. *That* is my problem. At a time when all could be and *is* heard and read—I just go about our lives babbling away.

*

Waves of jealousy. They are horrible to me. I've lived my whole life without being a slave to it, except for once. Just once and that lasted a relatively short time.

    But with you—it could cause me to become stark raving mad. It's like you said—I remember a thing you have said and it just goes around and around in my head and I torture myself. You have nothing to do with it—because I know you would never want me to feel this way—as I would never want you to have a moment of misery. So I'm going to try very, very hard to make it stop. No, I couldn't bear to see a picture of Deanna, because I would never be able to stop thinking of her, because I'm sure she was extraordinary, and I know you were crazy in love with her, and I know that I am nothing like her. So I couldn't bear to have that image in my mind. You're lucky in that I was never attracted to physically beautiful people—except women— which was wonderful because I never wanted to sleep with them or fall in love with them in that all-encompassing way.

    So you could never look upon anyone from my past and think, "He's beautiful," because they were all strange-looking—even on the fringe of ugliness. I veered far, far away from beauty. I found it almost too alien for me—I gravitated toward scars and crooked teeth and malformed bones, gauntness. So being in love with a true, pure-to-the-point-of-scariness beauty is very difficult for me at times. So please bear with me—my jealousy is so young, so reckless—so new and strong, even overwhelming. I don't know why it exists when we love each other so much—you say it's the nature of it—and you told me how you hated being with Domini—and that whole situation sounds so miserable and yet it makes me feel better?? That you two were miserable makes me feel better. Why is that? It's crazy.

To know that I would never change anything about myself—the way I look, the way I think—the way my life has gone (except for not being with you). I wouldn't change anything so why am I jealous? Because someone else got a piece of you or had an impact on you.

So, I'm going to try really, really hard to stop it. I think it's corrosive. I do.

I want you to try, too. For you have nothing to ever be jealous of—even though most of the time that reasoning means nothing.

Damien . . . you just called . . . you said something to me that I will never forget, and it means so much to me—more than you even know. You said that you have never been happy until now. I thought my heart would just burst.

You, my dear, have made me happier than I have ever been—and I know we both suffer not being able to be together. But to hear something like that makes all of my "suffering" worth it.

*

Do you remember one of the first times we ever spoke on the phone—the second time, actually. I started whispering to you—and you said . . . "Why are you whispering?"

It's so funny, it just seemed the right way to speak to you.

Now we do it all the time.

Yes, you are definitely turning into me, I am turning into you.

*

Not to be a nagging lover, but just how much are you smoking these days? On my next visit, I'm going to come back there and have a little chat with all of those who continue to send you cigarettes as a gift. And what's this about cigars??!! You thought I was going to let that slide, didn't you? Well, guess again. Maybe you should take to chewing sugarless gum.

*

Damien, we do talk of sanity, insanity a lot—but I honestly do believe you are the sanest person I have ever known. You're honest and I think to most people, the truth sounds like the ravings of a madman.

But I want you to know—I have never thought of you as insane. I think we're both a little "off"—but even then—I don't think we are—we are more aware of who we are and what we are doing than anyone I've ever encountered. Think of all the crazy things people around us do—and yet, they look at us like we are crazy.

Yours, forever and ever,

Lorri

February 10, 1997

My love,

You should get a package at the same time as this letter, so I will explain it.

1. The coffee—for the short period that I tried to drink coffee, this was the kind I drank.
2. The "Breakfast drink"—I drink a glass of this every day. Look at all the vitamin C in it!
3. The spoon—I have these lying around everywhere, because they give me one 3 times a day and I never throw them away.
4. The oatmeal cake—when I eat one of these, I can't stop. I will eat 4 or 5 of them.
5. The pack of oatmeal—I buy boxes of this all the time; it has all different flavors in it, and I like them all.
6. The crackers—I love, love, love these. Yummy.
7. The red pen—I used this to underline things in books.
8. The black pen—I have used this pen many times to write to you.
9. The strawberry candy—you never know what kind you will get when you order this, because they have all different kinds and they send you whatever kind they want.

From now on, I will be forever looking for things to send you. Everywhere I go (where am I going besides to take a shower twice a week?) I will be looking for things to steal for you.

I love and belong to only you for eternity,

Damien

February 12, 1997

My dearest,

I love the gifts you sent me—now the pen you used to write to me is being used by me to write to you. I love this pen. I will use the red pen to underline things. I ate the oatmeal cake tonight—it was completely lalishla! And I will have the oatmeal and the coffee for breakfast. I will save the breakfast drink for Friday. The spoon I will keep with me all the time to stir my coffee and the crackers I will have tomorrow for a snack at work. I want to ask you about the small wooden coffin that arrived with the book. I put the strawberry candies in the coffin—but they didn't want to stay in there, so I took them out. I couldn't tell if the coffin didn't want the candy or the candy didn't want to be in the coffin. Where did you get it and what is it for?

*

You don't know how much I love these gifts!

I love you and am yours through eternity,

Lorri

February 28, 1997

My beautiful one,

Our 1-year anniversary? How can a whole year have passed
already? But then, in a way, it seems as if so much more time than
that has passed. It seems somehow much shorter and much longer
than one year. How can that be?

*

Yes, my love, we will be together, and it does not matter if it is while
living or in death. Either way, we will be together, so what does it
matter? We have eternity together, so this small amount of time that
we are separated must not be allowed to make us sad, because it
really means nothing. I feel so wonderful just thinking of it. Yes, my
love, we can endure this for now, because everything is ahead of us.
I am your ghost. No, I do not doubt at all! I have no doubts, my love.
I feel it deep inside of me, it's so huge it feels as if I will explode. I
will never again fear losing you, I will never fear anything because I
know that I have you.

I love you beyond measure,

Damien

February 28, 1997

My dearest love,

Damien, I can't spend another summer here—I have to get down to New Orleans. I got my last huge phone bill today. We can be strong, you and I—when we need to. There will be plenty of time for overindulgence. I have been quite proud of us. It makes me feel really good—like we are accomplishing something. OK if we talk once a day through the week and 4 times on Sat and Sunday—that's only $200.00—we can do that—yes—yes—yes!

And maybe I can come visit you more.

I love you,

Lorri

March 3, 1997

My dearest love,

   No, my love, you truly don't belong here. But neither do I. Just
hang on for a little longer, and I promise you that we'll go to where
we do belong. We'll go to nowhere. And you'll never have to worry
about this place again. Until then, just remember that I love you.

                                        Yours for eternity,

                                                      D.

March 27, 1997

My dearest:

I am beginning to think I will suffer almost as horribly as you will in your quest to give up cigarettes.

You are breaking my heart—when you called tonight—crying and saying that no matter what you can never do enough. Do you know how it makes me feel? I can't even begin to explain it to you. It's like everything is in vain. I know how you feel now when I ask questions—and you said, "Either you believe I belong to you or you don't and that's it." Well, either you believe that I can't live without you, and you are the meaning for me to be alive, and I love you more every day—and therefore all you need to do is let everything be—just let it happen. How many times have you told me that?

Sometimes I think we are the same person—sometimes I know exactly how you feel—I've felt those exact things. How do you survive it? I wonder how much of it is a strain on you from withdrawal? It kills me that you have to go through this—it does. It kills me if it takes you away from me—even for a minute.

You must always remember, Damien—my life is over without you. I will cease living. Now, I can't stop crying. Can we stop hurting each other? Can't we just hold each other so close in our hearts and just find the strength in that? That's what I have always done.

I keep going over in my head what have I done to make him feel this way?

Was it talking about Domini? Was it being upset about the

football player comment? Or maybe you want to pull away—
because I can't. I have always told you if anything ever happened to
us it would be because you leave me.

Please stop. Please stop doubting—it really does cause me so
much pain.

You couldn't know how much I acknowledge what you do
for me.

It is I who could never, ever do enough for you.

To be quite honest—I feel I don't even fit into hardly any of your
life . . .

All this stuff has been going on—everyone else knows about it.
That guy from Baton Rouge going to see Domini. You arranging
with the little people to talk to her so that you might see Seth . . .

A whole world has been happening that I know nothing about.
Everyone around you—all these things they are doing for you and
they're all connected to you—and I'm here. I'm nothing and now
you say you feel me pulling away. When you doubt me it makes me
feel even more invisible.

I am so sad. How could you doubt me?

How could you?

After everything we've been through—after everything that has
happened.

Maybe you want me to go away.

Maybe you want your life back.

Maybe you want the simplicity of Domini—maybe you just don't
want to tell me.

You can't just call me up and do that to me—you can't. Because
all I can think now is—he doubts me, he has lost faith, he has lost
love.

Hence, I am forever lost.

How can you doubt us? How can you doubt this one thing we have been given in this life . . . this one hope?

I must stop.

No matter what you think—I love you and you will always own my soul.

Lorri

April 1, 1997

My Dearest Love,

No, I didn't think you were crazy, but now I know that you are. What is all this garbage about me doubting you or doubting us? Where the hell did that come from? Lorri, I never doubted you, I never doubted us. You started jumping to conclusions that I never even saw coming. How could you even think such a thing? How could you let that idea even enter your mind?

And all the talk about me pulling away from you, or wanting a "simple" life??!!! What the fuck?! Lorri, how could I ever even think of pulling away from you? You are my life, you are everything I live for, and everything I've ever been through was bringing me to you, there is nothing outside of you, so how could I pull away? I don't understand it. And how could life without you be simple? Before you came, my life was agony, it was a living hell, because I didn't have you—so how can you call that simple?

I was trying to explain that no words could ever express how much I love you, and that no action I could ever perform could demonstrate how much you mean to me—and you think I'm trying to pull away from you?! I was crying because there was no way for me to show you what you do to me, how you make me feel, how overcome I was by what I feel for you, and you think I want to get away from you.

Lorri, don't you understand that you are my life? Without you, I am nothing. I live only for you. And if you believe any of those things you said, even for a second, then you had to believe that everything between us was a lie.

Baby, I have no life without you. I would end this life in a split second if I didn't have you. Lorri, without you it would all be over. There would be no reason to continue with anything. We are linked body and soul, and if I were separated from you, I would curl up and die.

I don't want to ever hear of you thinking, feeling, or saying anything like that ever again. I have given you my life, my heart, and my soul, I belong to you, Lorri. If you ever think otherwise, then you're fooling yourself. I love you, Lorri Davis—not for 100 years, or 1,000 years, I mean for eternity. And don't you ever forget it, and don't you ever doubt it.

When I thought of your words, I panicked. I felt like my heart was about to explode. Lorri, please—you must believe that I am yours, that I love you beyond measure. You are all I live for.

Please believe it, never doubt it, I love and belong to you for

eternity,

Damien

April 1, 1997

Dearest,

Damien, do you realize how strong it is between us? Oh, of course you do—no one in the world makes love as wonderful as we do. And right now it's our imaginations—but then, what could be more divine? My only boundary is my words, my vocabulary—but I really can feel everything and I can imagine how everything would feel—but my favorite thing to do lately is to imagine how things would feel to you.

*

When I first moved to New York—I found an apartment on 88th Street. It was the fifth floor (a walk-up)—I've told you about that place. Well, I had no desire to be with anyone. I was so happy to be with myself only. It was summer and in that apartment it was about 100 degrees every night. I've always been very "erotically minded"—meaning I've always kind of been turned on by myself—never by anyone else—or anything else—until now—and the match was well worth the wait and the preparation. Anyway . . . my bedroom had a huge window, which faced a bank of apartment buildings.

So, every night, I would walk around in my apartment, completely nude—with my hair piled up on the top of my head—sometimes I would purposefully do things like bend over to pick something up off the floor facing away from the window, of course, and sometimes I would absentmindedly be touching myself in front of the mirror—or put on lotion—anything. I loved the thought of someone watching me. I loved it. Anyone, man or woman. I didn't even think about who—just as long as I made them crazy—and I didn't even really exist for anyone but myself (and you).

Damien . . .

I didn't really do that. I just thought it up and thought it sounded kind of erotic—but only if the person watching me were you and you didn't know who I was yet—that drives me crazy—and every night you came a million times while watching me. And you were silent, like me.

*

There is something very, very exciting to me—the thought of those not worthy of you looking at you and maybe wanting you—and I know you are mine. It does something to me—it is a double-edged sword—my jealousy makes me crazy that they would even consider looking upon you, yet there's some other part of me that glows within knowing how precious and beautiful you are and completely irresistible—and you are all mine—and I am all yours—and no one could make me feel the way you do.

To be quite honest—I did walk around nude all the time—but I had a curtain—well, a sheet on my window.

How do you feel about that? About someone looking at me and wanting me—do you hate it or love it or both?

Forever,

Lorri

April 7, 1997

My love,

   Tonight, I have decided that I will start doing push-ups and sit-ups every day. I did them for a while, then I just quit. It's very hard. It's not the actual exercise that's hard, it's finding the motivation. It bores me to death. There's a billion other things I would rather do. But this time I will try to stick to it.

*

My beautiful creature, we're going to build a lot more history together, so I guess you will just feel more "solid" every day. We are going to build a history that stretches to infinity.

   Lorri, don't think about the "homesick" feeling now. Just remember that we'll be going home soon, just us, and we will never leave again, and we never have to let anyone in. Forever.

   Lorri, I love Johnny Cash and Willie Nelson.

   And I love you.

I belong to you for eternity,

D.

P.S. I still say that if we ever get married, I want your last name.

May 2, 1997

My dearest, dearest Damien,

Something very scary just happened—
My doorbell rang—you know how I get . . .
I hid in the bathroom til they went away. Later, Luis came home and he said—"What's this?"
Roses. Left at the door. I was completely freaked out. No note. Nothing. Damien, it scared me. I called Susan. I said, please take these, let them be for you, let them be for you—take them away!!
Later she called, she said, "Lorri, I found a note. They are for me."
I laughed and laughed. I was so happy.
Things like that terrify me.
If I would've opened the door and there was some man there standing with roses, I would've screamed.

I love you,

L.

May 13, 1997

Miss L.,

Would you meet me tonight at exactly midnight, so that I may fuck you? If you do not have a previous engagement to attend, I would be delighted to slither my way in between your legs and thrust myself up inside you while running my tongue down your throat to muffle your cries. Or, if you would prefer, I could lie flat on my back so that you could sit over my mouth and feel me licking you, tasting you, while at the same time taking me into your mouth and causing me to come with your exquisite beautiful lips. Actually, Miss L., I am open to any suggestion you may have as to how to pass a delightful evening in your presence. As you may well know, you are in possession of my absolute and total love, and that I am always yours.

Yours to command in this and all matters,

D.

June 30, 1997

My love,

Seeing you these last two days did something to me. Everything was different. Everything seems a little easier now. I don't know how to explain it. But I like it. I feel like I can deal with things easier and better now. Now I can relax and just allow things to flow as they should.

I believe you were more beautiful this time than I've ever seen you look before. I would have given anything to touch you. Lorri, I do pay attention to the things you wear, I notice every little thing about you, don't think I don't. I think it's cute that you think about what you're going to wear. I love that. And I definitely love the way you look in those pants you wore on Thursday. You have no idea how good your ass looks. You are perfect in every way. I love to look at you.

I saw a psychiatrist when I was in high school, too. He said, "For the love of hell, lock that thing away."

As for what Susan said about people down here not living together before they get married—what's the point in it? If you're going to live together, where's the sense in getting married? I see none.

*

Lorri, you're moving to Little Rock!!! We will only be a few minutes apart!! It's like I can't even comprehend it yet, it's too big to process. Everything's going to change so much. I just love to think about it. And so soon!

I am yours,

Damien

July 10, 1997

My love: I just arrived in Little Rock—neither Mara nor Linda is
home yet, so I'm sitting on the front porch swing, writing to you. I
was listening to the country music station you listen to, hoping
against hope you were listening to it, too.

Damien—I do believe our love is everything to you. I can just be
so petty sometimes. All the things that we've been talking about
seem so pointless—so vapid—when we should only be so, so happy
that we have each other. I want to keep you so much to myself—I'm
such a baby. But accept anything and everything that happens. I just
want to understand why you do the things you do. All my life I've
wanted to understand things—that's why religion was so puzzling to
me—I couldn't understand why people felt the need for it—that one
I figured out very quickly. But you, you do things and I want to
know why—I want to know why you do everything. You speak
sometimes of how I seem to be running around in circles tearing my
hair out—I suppose if I could find another way to express myself
you wouldn't get caught up in all of that and I could find out what I
want (need) to know. Because when we start in—it's awful and I
can't follow you and I know at times you don't follow me and most
of the time I just want to understand something. My curiosity has
nothing to do with doubt of your love for me or of our destiny or
my love for you. As I have said so many times—I could never doubt
any of that. Never.

But sometimes, you take it in that way, and I can understand—

especially when I'm being childish or jealous or possessive. As you know, those feelings are so caustic to me—I want to fix that somehow. Or at least make it easier. I just want to love you, I just want to make you happy—I don't want you to feel that I'm anything but right there with you, all the time, holding you. So I'm going to pay a lot more attention to what you say and how I say things. I don't want to do that anymore, hurt each other. It's true what you said—the deeper our love gets—the more intense everything gets. It's so powerful and not to be trifled with.

It is so quiet in this city. I like the street they live on—there's no one around. I wish I could just live on this street. Never have to look anywhere else. Do you know I really would like to get a job at a library . . . no, I want to keep drawing. It's what I like to do. You know I would've gotten to you in 6½ hours today. I can't believe I haven't asked, but I wonder if it would be possible to make 2 appointments to see you if they are not consecutive days. Then I could've seen you today and Friday. Could things be so civilized?

There are lots of cats around here. I hope Cretin forgives me, wherever he is.

*

I feel so different when I am here, so close to you, so close to where you are physically. Damien, I can really tell a difference. I am much calmer, feel quiet, assured. I know you don't understand Mara but being around her makes me feel good—I feel something reassuring in her, too. Possibly because she actually knows you and cares for you and respects what we are, enough not to ask me questions—but I can tell she knows it's something very, very strong. I like it, too, that she's older than I am—I have always liked being around people that are older than me. Especially if they are smart—which she is—and intuitive and have done a lot in their life. I must say, I don't usually take advice—because even in times of duress, I know I will find my answer—but I like to hear other people's perceptions of things.

I love to take advice from you though. You are the first soul I have ever listened to. I wish sometimes you would give me more—'cause I love to hear what you think of my predicaments. I also love to give you advice. I love it, love it, love it. Because it means so much to me when you ask—I think about those things for days when you ask—even though I know my first inclination is the right one.

So . . . now that I have calmed down . . .

How would you feel if someone was concerned about your effect on me? Would dare question it—when it is beyond anything they could imagine and their little mind is making a judgment of you—for my sake—when I belong to you—have been wedded to you for all time—

I know even thinking of it seems silly—but how would you feel about that person?

So, you see—that's what I was trying to see all that time. It's kind of like some idiot trying to take apart or pass judgment on the purest form of beauty—the purest—whatever its shape or content—but absolute perfection. I mean I know in a way that the idiot is made even more stupid—or ignorant—by even trying to question or take apart the pure beauty—like it even has the right to look at it—and that in itself should be enough to make it nothing—but at the same time, wouldn't you just love to poke its eyes out for even daring to look upon pure perfection (which it can't even perceive)?

*

Well, I hope I have made myself clear. You know of who I speak. Now maybe you understand.

I always will.

*

I wish my travel thru my various states didn't have to take a toll on you—but Damien, most of the time I am so ecstatic, I am so happy to have you—even when I am crying or confused, I am still happy to have you. You must know that and know that every little thing I conquer really does make me stronger and soon I won't have to fight anymore—for I will have you in my arms. And I will rest.

Yours forever,

Lorri

July 24, 1997

My Beautiful Love,

We just got off the phone, and I have been thinking. Beautiful one, I am never going to make a decision for you. I think that if you want to go to Egypt, then you should. You said you used to like going places like that. Maybe you still would. You must make these decisions. No my love, don't look at anything for me. The last time I saw Egypt was either in 1932 or '36, I can't remember which. But it had been ruined, even then. It was once a powerful, beautiful place.

I am yours for eternity,

Damien

August 5, 1997

My dearest:

I want so much to be strong for you—but today was one of the
hardest things I have ever encountered—seeing you, the way they
had you all chained up—being so close to you, not being able to
touch you—none of this makes any sense to me. I can't even talk to
you; if I could just hear your voice—hear how you are.*

Damien—this day is so awful. When you looked back at me with
those eyes of yours. All I wanted to do was run up there, throw my
arms around you. How is it possible to live in a world that is so, so
cruel? I couldn't even think all the way home—I felt like my mind
was a wasteland. I felt so, so wrung out—and everything was so
surreal. I got to meet your mother; she took hold of my hand and
didn't let go—I didn't want her to let go, because she had just
touched you. She told me they were trying to get me back to see
you. I talked to Ron briefly—he said the same thing. But at least I
was in the same room with you. At least I had that. I got to look at
you for a few minutes. I was OK or I thought I was OK for some of
the day. I felt similar to the way I felt the first time I saw you—it just

---

* This was a Rule 37 hearing for Damien to be appointed a new counsel, ordered
by a judge, as part of his appeal process; the Rule 37 is the procedure to prove that
the original trial attorneys were ineffective, and that effective representation would
have resulted in a different outcome. It was Damien's first time outside of prison in
three years—he was painful to look at, dressed in prison whites, hair unkempt, and
shackles around his wrists, ankles, and waist. He was terribly thin.—LD

feels like something has been ripped out of me. Like I had been suddenly starved or depleted of any nutrient or moisture in my entire body. I got home and laid on my bed for a while and then it all came out like a wave of sickness—I couldn't cry hard enough. I cried for a solid hour nonstop. I cried until I was gagging and sick— choking on my own tears. I cried till I was so exhausted—but I had to do it. I had to get it all out because it just hurts too much sometimes and today—even though I wouldn't have wanted to be anywhere else in the world—it was torture, though. But I still wouldn't have missed it for that one look from you. I would've driven 16 hours for that one look.

*

Today, after I stopped crying—I decided to start thinking of everything we've done together. There is so much. It made me really, really calm and happy. How well I know you, how much I have come to depend on you, and I am glad of it. I completely depend on you and you never, ever let me down—you are always there—and I am always here for you.

*

Damien, what you were saying about feeling things—and how you never have before . . . it is because of us—everything that happens to you or me is because of us. It's so wonderful even though sometimes it hurts so much, or it leaves us "stunned" but just think how amazing it all is . . . Damien, you are so powerful to me and for me—you have the ability to do anything to me—I feel things and know things. Soon, we will touch each other. I know it.

I love you, I belong to you,

L.

August 14, 1997

My love,

   I am going to try to get someone to call and tell you, but I
figured I should send this just in case—once again, they have put a
block on your phone. I knew this was going to happen. I will talk to
you as soon as I can. I miss your beautiful voice so much already. I
know this is going to drive me insane. I love you, and that's all that
matters. Just hold that in your heart and repeat it over and over
again. I love you beyond measure.

                                        I am yours for eternity,

                                                    D.

August 19, 1997

My love,

I'm starting to feel something I've never felt in my life. I feel your protectiveness. I feel you wanting to protect me and I love it. Damien, it's so, so romantic to me. Not jealousy, it's absolute protectiveness of something that is yours. Yours to protect. I can't even believe how I feel now. And this is going to sound so, so funny, but I don't know how else to put it—but at times, you are the epitome of maleness to me. The way you look at me, how you say things to me, even when you don't realize it—it is the most natural feeling for me with you, whatever that thing is—male/female and any other word that encompasses the idea—whatever that is—it is the strongest it has ever been with you and me. I want you to take care of me, I want you to look at me the way you do. Like you own me, like I am yours, or when you look at me like you love the way I look at you. It makes me so, so much more in love with you each time.

And today, when I saw you—when you sat back against the wall and I could see all of you—Damien, I have never seen anything so beautiful—not just seeing all of you, or most of you—all at once—it's seeing you in that state of what your love for me does to you—what my love for you does to you.

But then there was this sudden desire in me—I wanted you to see me. I wanted it, but something else said, "Not all of you, just a little." I don't know why—I could've taken off all my clothes right then and there.

212

*

I was thinking of what you said about buying clothes for your trial—
and in the rest of our life together. I will always want to get things
for you. I've been thinking of what I would get for you. Different
things every time.

*

I went out to stand in the vacant lot across from where I live to look
at the moon. It is so incredibly beautiful tonight.

Did you make the moon water? I can't wait to drink it with you.

*

Damien . . . I just got a job.

I love you so much,

Lorri

September 11, 1997

My beautiful wife,

Yes, my beautiful one, I am so happy that they are going to let you take time off from work to come here. But it's only natural, don't you think? Everything else has fallen into place, so this must also. It couldn't be otherwise. And now I see you in 4 days! I can't wait.

*

The [dentist] came down here today and he stopped to talk for a couple of minutes. He says he wants to write my biography. I just stood there and looked at him. I don't have time for any such nonsense. It would be impossible to do such a thing—my attention is completely and totally held by you. And it makes me angry that people can't realize it. There is no room for anything but you.

*

Yep, now I outweigh you by 34 pounds. Now I want to lie on top of you while I'm inside of you, and hold you down so that you couldn't move a muscle even if you wanted to. And that's how I want to fuck you. And I will keep my mouth clamped over yours, so that you can't even cry out. Is that what you still want?

I am yours forever,

Damien

September 19, 1997

My love,

It's strange, isn't it, that dentist who wants to write your
biography? I suppose if anyone were going to write it—a dentist is
the best choice. Can you imagine a biography from a dentist's point
of view?

"At about the age of 12 a catastrophic event . . . 14 cavities all at
once! This was a direct result of the lifestyle she had fallen into.
Cakes, cookies, ice cream. Her life was a whirl of treats and good-
time boys. 2 of which did not receive cleanings every 6 months and
were from the wrong side of the tracks . . ."

He would write about you based on the condition of your
teeth . . .

Years of smoking—suddenly halted, a sweet tooth, if not teeth—
one could write a book based on the condition of his mouth . . .

I'm not really grasping the dental/biography thing.

I think it's kind of funny, though.

Although I completely know what you mean about not having
space for anything else . . .

Going to work drives me crazy. I hate to have to think of
anything but you.

Yours forever and yours alone,

L.

October 6, 1997

Dear Mrs. Echols,

I like saying that. And I will now be able to say it for all eternity.

Lorri, I don't think you know how very happy you have made me this day. Yes, my beautiful one, I am certain, 100% positive, beyond a shadow of a doubt, without question—I want to be married to you. I want it as much as I want to have a child with you—it's on the same level to me. They are two of the most beautiful things that I can conceive of. I want them with you. I want them so much. I can think of nothing more beautiful.

*

I can't stop thinking of it. It's all I can think of. Lorri, we are going to be married!!! Is that not a miracle? Is that not magick?

My beautiful one, what I was talking about on the phone—what I did is called "The Invocation of the Four Watchtowers"—fire, air, earth, and water. All it is is a highly concentrated prayer to invoke all 4 elements to fill you with their spirit. It's just like receiving the Eucharist. In essence, it is a way of saying to the magick, "Fill me, make me one with you." I haven't done it in years. And when I did it, I felt the binding. You kept asking who did it—there were these idiots that are so pompous, so full of themselves, that they believe things like that are their "job," their "responsibility." If they thought I was the one that had killed those children, and that it was for some magickal purpose, as everyone said, then they would have done it to keep me from harming anything else with magick—at least that's what they say. The truth is that they do it to save face, to distance themselves from me, because they feel that any action I performed could reflect badly on them. I should have expected such a thing long ago, but I wasn't even here one week when I received a letter telling me how I had single-handedly set the entire movement of magick-users and witches back at least 500 years, and how they had worked so hard to clear up stereotypes, misconceptions, and superstitions commonly held, and I had wrecked it all. No, there is no way to remove it—only the one who did it can remove it—but there are thousands of ways around it. Whoever did it is not very strong. It seems like something a common witch would do.

I am yours for eternity,

Damien

October 6, 1997

Damien, your face is not fat.

It is so, so beautiful. There is not an ounce of fat on you. You are perfect. And so incredible to look at—every time I see you, I am amazed at how much more beautiful you have become.

Something incredible has happened. You want to marry me. Damien, I was so afraid that you wouldn't want to. I am in awe to think that you will be my husband. I have never spoken those words, "my husband." My husband, Damien.

I want so to please you, always—to make you feel how enormous this all is to me. How much I respect you for how you believe. That's what I mean . . . I have always felt I would live without it if you felt it wasn't right. But I am thrilled to know that you want it— please tell me again that you believe it can and will be sacred between us. That you can feel that way with me. I can't regret anything in my life—I can only know everything brought me to you—but you must always remember, I have never given myself in marriage. I have never called anyone "my husband." It doesn't matter—all that matters to me is that you love me.

I live to be by your side, forever,

Lorri

October 7, 1997

My beautiful lover,

Lorri, I do want to be married to you. I want it so badly. Every
time I think of it, I feel light-headed. Yes, I want it. It will make
everything so much better, and it will put an extra barrier around us,
so that nothing could even begin to come into our world. Baby, it's
going to be absolutely perfect. Nothing could be more divine. I can
hardly wait for it. It's going to be so perfect, and so right. Lorri,
don't you doubt that I want it, even for a second. I want it. It is
something of us.

I love and belong to you for eternity,

D.

October 16, 1997

My Beautiful Lover,

The moon is really bright out there, and I'm making the water. It's so cold in here, my bones are hurting, and I love it. Fall is here at last.

I knew you could tell how I was feeling, the meanness, as soon as you picked up the phone. And it has only gotten stronger as the night progresses.

*

Baby, don't you think I have seen all that weakness you have left behind—like the self-pity—don't you think I can see it? You have truly amazed me, doing some of those things, because you have done it and not even looked back or relapsed. You become stronger with every ordeal we pass through. Lorri, I can see it very plainly. I don't think I become stronger, I think I have just become a little more wise, I have my eyes open a little more. You never stop teaching me. But I still have so, so far to go. And you will take me there.

*

Lorri—I have to get you a wedding ring!!! And yes, my love, you will have that dress. It will all work out. You have made me so happy. When I think of it, I can't even sit still.

I love you,

D.

October 29, 1997

My Beautiful One,

For the past two days, I have made love to you while I wait for
you to get home. . . .The reason I am able to live for a day, because I
know at the end of that day, I get to hear you tell me you love me.
That is what I live for.

I need you so much. I need you, need to just hear your voice so
very bad tonight. I miss you so bad, it is painful. It is hurting. I just
need to be near you, to hear you, to be able to tell you I love you.

Lorri, do you exist only for me? I just need to hear it. I need to
hear it. I need to hear you tell me that you cannot live without me,
that I am your life. I just need to hear it.

My lover, don't you realize you are all of those things to me? You
are perfect, and so, so beautiful, and you are the most magickal thing
that has ever existed. Lorri, you are the reason I live. You are my life,
my soul. I cannot draw a single breath without you. Please, please
tell me that you know these things, that you believe these things.
Please tell me, because if you do not know these things, then I will
lose my mind. I could not stand the pain of knowing that you did not
believe it with all your heart. Please tell me you know these things.
Lorri, I do worship you. I love you beyond my ability to express. You
must know that. I must make you see and understand. I must.

*

My lovely creature, you are my baby, and you already have 100% of
my attention, 24 hours a day. No one or nothing can take my

attention from you even for a second. So it's not even necessary for you to "cry out" for me to hold you, because that's what I am always doing.

Lorri, I want you to follow up what I say with something about you. I must hear those things, I must know how you are thinking and feeling, even if it's a reaction to something I have said. I must have that. Please, please don't stop.

*

I love you so much that I feel like my heart is breaking. I would give anything to hold you for just a moment right now. Anything. I love you so much. I only hope you can feel it. Lorri, I would not hurt you for anything. It kills me to know I've caused you pain. I love you so much. I belong to you, Lorri. And I'll do anything to prove it.

I am yours for eternity.

Damien

November 10, 1997

My beautiful Damien,

 Damien . . . sometimes I feel I should be doing more things to
help you. To find out things—just poking around some—it doesn't
seem like anyone else is—and I'm down here. I'm sure I could find
some stuff out. Just by asking questions around—following certain
people—looking at files, papers. I just feel like I'm wasting time. But
I want to have your support. I would be very, very careful. What do
you think? It certainly won't hurt. And I really don't see anyone else
doing anything.
 No, my lovely, I'll rephrase that—I don't feel I am wasting
time—I never do being with you. I just feel I could be doing
something that could quite easily be helpful in getting you out of
there. I think I could be a pretty good investigator.

*

Did you ever celebrate Thanksgiving? If so, how? I want to hear all
about it.
 This year, as it was last, you will be with me. As you always will
be from now on.
 I actually do make a dinner—but it's nothing anyone else would
want to eat. Namely you. We'll have to fix that—we'll come up with
the best meal from now on.

                                        Yours forever,

                                           Lorri

November 24, 1997

My love,

I've talked to you a hundred times today, and every single time I have forgotten to tell you that I am to see one of my attorneys tomorrow.

*

And I've been thinking about you being there with me through the entire trial next time. I just need to think this out, OK? You said as the time draws near, you think I will find it easier with you there. You are right, but I do not like it. I must think more on this.

And maybe you are right about us getting married—maybe it will just happen. But there's no use even thinking of it now, because our only chance is to wait and see. I don't mean not think of being married because it's so wonderful to think of it—I mean it's useless to think of when, where or how. If it is to happen, it will.

I am yours forever,

Damien

December 23, 1997

My Beautiful Wife,

I am now watching *Little Women*, but I can't stop thinking about
when we were talking earlier, and you have sent me a Christmas
present. And now I'm sad. Lorri, I want to give you something very
badly, but I do not have anything. The first Christmas that we are
together, you are going to wake up to find an entire room full of
things that I will bring for you. I promise.

You forgot to ask about the numerology when you were here on
Friday. Anyway, I don't remember much about it, because it was
something I barely even paid attention to. The main thing that I
remember is that I was looking at the chart one day, and I thought,
"If I have done this correctly, it means that I will be released within
my 23rd year." That's it.

And I do not want to hear even one more word about you being
fat. I refuse to hear another word of it.

I am going to go insane while you are in W. Virginia. I can feel it
beginning to set in already. It's a feeling of near panic. But I can
handle it. I have to. It's just three days. It'll be much better when we
go there together, but right now I am very jealous of that place.

I am yours forever,

Damien

December 29, 1997

My beautiful Damien,

   Damien, you must never feel sad because you think you don't
give me any presents—don't you know you give me everything I
could ever want every single day!?! You are the most miraculous gift.
I don't need or want anything else. Even when we are together, I still
just want you. There is nothing this world has to offer that I want.
Nothing. Just you, just your love. Anything else pales.

                              I love you, my darling,

                                            Lorri

February 5, 1998

My Dearest Damien:

This is going to be funny in a way—the first letter that I tell you all that has happened. Right now, I feel very, very down—for a lot of reasons, I think—because I can't talk to you anymore. But Julie called and talked to me for about an hour and I found her very depressing . . . Stuart calls me every day wanting to talk about the clothes he is wearing in Egypt—and all I want to do is to talk to you. All the other stuff just makes me want to go to sleep. It's funny, though, writing it down makes it seem "different."

*

It's so strange to me—these people, Julie, Susan, Stuart . . . well, not Susan so much—but the others. They will always ask about you— yet they know nothing, really. I mean Julie does somewhat and Stuart in another way—they just are always so respectful when they ask about you. Susan is different because anytime I talk to her, I am constantly talking about you—but sometimes she asks me things, she likes to ask me things about your legal situation, which I can't always answer.

Last night, when I told Linda—after a while she asked me what you (or we) were doing to prepare for your trial (!?).

She said . . . "You should get a copy of the transcript and go over every point together—make sure he has an answer to each and every one of them." She's very practical. But Damien, when that trial is approaching, we will do stuff like that—because I will stop at nothing to get you out of there.

I want to marry you more than anything, but this is what I mean when I say it has to be right, everything must be fixed.

My dad told me once, when my grandfather was still alive, they were very close—when he was going up to visit he would say, "Dad, I'll be up on Sunday." He wouldn't say, "I'll be there at 12:00 on Sunday" because he knew if he were late at all, my grandfather would fret and fret. Sometimes I do that with my dad, now. I don't tell him things that would worry him—there's no point, but to hurt him, cause him pain—I inherited my "anxiety" from him—not that it's an excuse, and I do want to fix it—especially now that it has been injected into you—but Damien, I will tell you everything, as if you were here living with me. And this is the start.

*

I just want everything to be where I want it to be, but I don't want to wait. But that has always been the way I am.

*

Damien, I can't wait to hear from these phone people . . . I get a nervous stomach (in a good way) whenever I think of being able to talk to you whenever we please. It will change our lives!! We could talk 2 hours on a Saturday! Make love, argue (and finish), tell stories—all of those things.

Yours forever,

Lorri

postscript, 2014

I made my first visit to Arkansas in the summer of 1996. So between phone calls, postage, and visits, by the fall of 1998 our relationship was taking a toll on my finances. But by that time, I had already made the decision to move south. I had no idea how my life was going to unfold; I just knew it lay in being closer to Damien and somehow playing a role in the fight for his freedom. I've always regarded that moment in time as when I switched to automatic pilot. I remained in that mode for a long, long time.

I had only experienced the small town where the prison was located in Tucker, Arkansas. I knew I would never survive living there, so my initial plan was to relocate to New Orleans. I thought it would be close enough to visit Damien on a regular basis, and I could still live an interesting, urban lifestyle. I needed to know that I could find good coffee and French movies.

I was wrong about New Orleans—I lived there for a month before it became clear that at seven hours away by car, it was too far. But before I left, there was one task I needed to undertake. Damien had been sending my letters to Rick in Baton Rouge, and I wasn't comfortable with a stranger having access to them. It was 1998, before I had a cell phone, so I stopped at a pay phone and called to let Rick know I was going to his home to pick them up. New Orleans is a strange, spooky, wonderful place, but Baton Rouge just seemed scary to me. Maybe it was the fear of going to an unknown man's house, who happened to be an undertaker. My gut was telling me to turn around, but I was determined to get my letters.

It turned out to be much easier than I expected. Rick was as polite as can be, and I remember even having a lovely chat with him. However, there seemed to be a sign from the gods, a sight I recall as clear as if it were yesterday: I saw a car burning on the side of the road. It was pitch-black, and not another soul on the interstate. I saw it for a while before I got right next to it, and as it became a spot on the horizon behind me. That fire was one of the eeriest sights I've ever encountered.

Shortly after my pilgrimage to Baton Rouge, I relocated once again to Little Rock, Arkansas, which turned out to be a lovely town with lots of big trees and Victorian houses. I set my sights on a beautiful brick 1856 row house with a porch swing, and within two years I would be living in one of the upstairs flats. The ceilings were fourteen feet tall, the windows were many and over seven feet tall, and it was surrounded by beautiful oak trees. I had a porch, had adopted some stray cats, and was soon at home in a very southern way.

I didn't know anyone, only a few people I had met at the prison on visitation. I managed to get a job in the city government as a park designer. No one at my new job knew anything about my connection to Damien, and as much as I disliked the undercurrent of lies that was forming in my life, I felt it was necessary in order to protect my privacy. I concocted a story that I was doing research about southern prisons for a documentary, thus setting up a weekly visit to Tucker. I managed my work hours around Damien time, and everything became about our schedule: daily phone calls, weekly visits, and the daily trip to the post office to mail letters.

It's hard to believe that my life would settle into a routine. I'd work through the week, then go see Damien on Fridays for three hours. We would talk every day; sometimes we'd go crazy and talk all day—both of us knowing we couldn't afford it, but somehow we managed.

Lorri

February 6, 1998

My Beautiful one,

I am including Fr. Charles's card. He and I just talked about him
performing our wedding ceremony, and he said that he could do it,
but there's a lot of paperwork and stuff that would have to be gone
through, an annulment. Anyway, he said it will take at least a year
to go through it all. He said to give you this card, and for you to
call him at the St. Judes number. We must talk more about this
tomorrow.

*

I love you so very much. My life is yours.

And I want to make love to you and hear you, too. But I think we
should wait for that new phone line. Then it will be better. I miss
hearing you. But I miss seeing you even more. I love you, Lorri.

You have once again said something that would never have
otherwise crossed my mind—about it being sad that our daughter
would never experience a love like ours. I didn't stop to think it was
sad, because I was so caught up in us. But now that you have drawn
my attention to it, it is sad.

And Lorri, I understand perfectly what you were saying earlier,
but it still hurts me, hearing you talk about those contact visits,
knowing how badly you want them, and knowing that I can't give
them to you. I would cut off my hands to be able to just kiss you.

Lover, sometimes I become scared because I think of being out
there with you, just living for and with you—then I look around me

and see where I am, and anything else seems too good to be true. I see these bars, and it sometimes feels that there will never, ever be a time when those bars are not there. You have no idea how that feels, what it's like. It's a nightmare that you can never wake up from. I can feel you so very close, I can hear, see, and even smell you—yet there is still a huge gulf between us, keeping me from reaching out and touching you. And then you must once again leave, and I must return to this burial chamber and continue to stare at these bars, thinking about what's so very close, but beyond my touch. Sometimes the only thing that gives me the strength not to collapse is to hear your words, your voice, promising me that our time will come. You are my light. I just want to live in you. I don't want to be touched by anything but you. You are my soul. I love you so much.

*

Lorri, I want you to be at those court hearings. It will be very scary without you there. I need you there. I've been thinking about the trial, too. I want you to come during the first few days, for the jury selection—but I don't want you there during the state's part—which is the first part—but I want you there during the defense. I was talking to Cally about it. We'll talk about it more when the time draws near.

I am yours for eternity,

D.

February 1998

Damien, now I am in London. I slept on the plane—7½ hours
to get here and now I have five hours to wait here in the airport. I
can't stop seeing your beautiful face everywhere I go. You told me to
concentrate on the thing about all of this that I like. Well, what I like
is thinking of you so that is what I do. That is what I like best about
this trip. And trying to stay happy that soon I will be back with you.
Nothing out in this world matters to me. Nothing. There is nothing
I can see or do that compares to how I feel when I hear your voice
or see you.

*

I knew this would happen . . . the more "away" physically I am
becoming, the closer I am feeling. And waves of emotion keep
sweeping over me. I am able to think of everything—but differently.
I do believe I will figure a lot out. I was just thinking of how angry
you were at me on Friday night—Damien, we have to fix that,
because I don't want to feel like this ever again—I know there are so
many things I don't understand, but you're right—never have you
talked to me with such anger, such resentment—I'm not
disregarding the situation—and I hate my reaction to you. Most of
the time I just don't know how to react, for I've never had to think
like that before . . . Maybe if you told me what it is that makes you
so angry—I know the obvious things, but when I asked you if I was
a part of your anger—I am not being whiny or trying to make you
feel bad—Damien, I want to fix it, I want to know what it is that has
seeped in—because it makes me angry, too. I don't want to hear you

like that as much as you don't want to be that way. But I have a lot to do, too. I want to take better care of us. You kept saying you couldn't afford for us to be that way before I left. Damien, we can never afford to be that way. I want to know and I want you to know everything that I feel. I want to hold you like you are the most precious treasure on this earth, because you are. And while I cannot control the stupidity that surrounds you and continues to grow—I can be to you what I want to be, what I need to be—everything that you need, everything that you want. Don't you know that's what I am? I hope that while I am away you decide that you want to be with me as much as I need to be with you. There's no question. I cannot live without you, but I don't want it to be this way.

*

I wish your mother would let me have some baby photographs of you—or when you were little. I would love to have them. Even just one. Do you think she would? Would it be wrong to ask her? Damien, I just want to have it. I've seen a photo of you . . . in that movie, there is a picture of you and your sister. I used to freeze the screen so I could see it—but I don't do that anymore.

*

Damien, I have just come from the Egyptian Museum and it truly has done something to me. All of those incredibly beautiful and magickal creatures. I have no doubt my love that you are of them. And after I saw Queen Tiye, who is the most beautiful woman and the face of Aka nation (sp?), I am so stricken. This is of you, purely of you, and even though it was like pulling teeth, thank you for allowing me to come here. For it is because of you. I know you feel so disappointed with this place now—there are things for me to learn and I would give anything to have you here with me, so I could learn. With you—I can do anything. As I walked through that place I never felt so sad, so loved, so happy, so beautiful—because I have you, because you are not far away from me and because I am coming home to you and more than everything—that I am going to marry you. And you are brilliant and beautiful and strong and mine.

*

It's 7:42, almost time to speak to you. Tonight I will make love to you. I have been thinking of you constantly, my love. Damien, life is not going to remain "easy" for us until we are together. We want each other too much—even this, me seeing these things without you, it's just not right.

Tonight, I was talking to an Egyptian woman. She asked if Stuart and I were friends or what. I said yes, for a long time. She asked if I was married or in love. I said I was very much in love and then she said, "He is not jealous?" I said, "Yes, very much so, but not of Stuart (exactly)—other things." She said, "Would you not be jealous if he went with a woman on a trip?" Oh Damien, it made me think, of course! I said, "I could never stand it, I would be out of my mind with jealousy." Why have I been so stupid? My place is with you, never, ever with anyone else. I just know when we are living together, we will never be parted. Never, ever. It kills me to think how foolish I have been, I will make it up to you. I will, in so many ways. I am only devoted to you.

*

Just now, at 8:00, I put my hands on the rail in the bathroom, spread my legs standing up, on my toes, and felt you fucking me. It was the loveliest thing of the day. I hope you were doing the same.

Damien, I have so much to learn, I am only beginning. Words have been going through my head, like "beloved" and "loving desperately." I like to think of you as my beloved, for you are. And as far as being "desperately in love" I feel that at times, too. I think it stems from not being able to touch you.

*

It's Wednesday night. As each day goes by, I feel the weight on my heart grow lighter, as I get closer to you. At times I feel . . . what an incredible experience, but it isn't without you. No one could ever understand but you that nothing means anything and I can't feel anything without you. I can only hope you will want to hear about things I have done, or read these pages.

One thing that I haven't been able to stop thinking about is that I have been given a gift, Damien; the main purpose, the only purpose of my life is that I will be able to free you and love you, to live with you and have a child with you who will spread magick throughout her life. We just have to trust and hold on to that trust and love through the "tough times" and I mean the times we want each other so much that we could literally claw each other to death—I want, I need to be more careful, to be more careful of your heart, because it tears me apart to see the effects things have on you. You are so very precious to me and I have made some seemingly bad decisions, but I always come around to where I need to be.

Please know you are my life. Without you, I cease to live. I know this missive will be all over the place, jumping from thought to thought, from emotion to emotion, from place to place, from day to day. But I write anytime I get a spare second.

*

Today, a Muslim woman pulled me aside to tell me the importance of marriage. She told me that an Egyptian man marries only once, forever. Well, I told her that is the only true marriage—forever, nothing else is marriage, but how many wives does an Egyptian man have? Which, of course, was not the thing to say, but I will not be lectured when she has no idea what love is. No one can talk to me about it.

*

Thursday morning. I didn't sleep at all last night—the nights are very hard for me—things come after me, will not leave me in peace—I tried to seek some peace reading *Sandman*—but it scared me even more. I am like a little girl, afraid of the dark, when morning comes I am all right. It is not good for me. It comes from being so far away from you. Last night my heart was beating so strongly. Several times I just sat up in bed, looked around me, wondered where I was. I was almost delirious. Yes, during the days I am stronger—and I am getting closer. I hope you are faring well, my love. I think of you constantly. I hope you are eating and sleeping and I hope you have peace of mind and are waiting for my return— as I am counting the minutes. If I find out when I get home that you have put another of your spells on me to make me miserable and not be able to sleep, I am going to wring your little neck. If I find out you've done this to me again, which after last night's bout with the ghosts and how my heart was pounding—you will pay dearly, my little man. Don't you think for a moment I am not capable of the same, however, it will be something else entirely. And if I arrive home and don't find amongst my many missives from you a Valentine's message, more wrath will come your way. I mean it.

I don't care, you have already spoilt me with last year's beautiful card.

*

You thought life with me was going to be easy. Well. It's not. But I promise it will be sublime.

*

Friday night. I was so sick today. My sweet, I will never, ever ever call you a baby again. I had forgotten how bad it feels to throw up, not be able to eat or drink anything. It was food poisoning. That has never happened to me before. I was able to get up later in the day; I wanted to see the temple at Luxor and the Karnak temple because they were so huge. I love looking at things that are that huge. Now I am so tired.

*

Do you realize next week is 2 years since I found you? My beloved, my life, my heart, my soul.

*

Tomorrow I go back to Cairo at 6:00 in the morning—even if I wasn't so in love with you, I would be hard-pressed to ever travel with Stuart again. I am completely exhausted. But my love for you is strong and that alone will get me through.

*

It's Sunday night. I saw a beautiful church today that made me feel so close to you. All day today I was puzzled by you and what you are. This land does that to me—I am confused. With your Seth and your magick and your gods and your beliefs. I feel you in all of these things. And I am confused today about what your love for me is . . . how it manifests itself in so many ways it seems. I would go through so many feelings today. I have had a day of mosques and churches and bazaars and falafel for dinner—nothing, nothing of me. That will happen tomorrow in England. That is a place I want to be with you. Damien, I am and will continue to be vexed by you. I will spend my life figuring it out. At this moment, I have so many questions for you . . . I want to understand so much, I want you to tell me your thoughts—I want to know what you want.

*

Damien . . . it's Monday morning finally and I am on a plane from Cairo to London. All of the wishing in the world will not make this plane go any faster, nor will it make it fly straight to the United States.

I keep thinking of lovers who have been separated for years without a look, without a word—and right now I feel so fortunate in that in a few hours I will hear you again. All I want to do is talk to you about pure silliness. Anything that you've done this week. Anyone that you have seen or talked to, what you watched, any movies. I suppose this little booklet will tell you what I have been doing.

*

I can hardly believe it . . . I am on a plane bound for the United States. I'm not quite there yet, but still, just sitting here, I feel better.

*

My love: I will finish this little book of words and nonsense and—I don't even know what else. I love you more than you know, Damien. And I am anticipating hearing your voice.

Forever yours,

Lorri

February 1998

My dearest beloved,

Every time you come back, I always forget how it is when you are gone, like a woman who can no longer remember the pain of giving birth. When you are away, it always seems as though you never really even existed, like a sliver of my childhood wishes that fade away once I awaken. It's like trying to hold on to a handful of smoke. You paw the air frantically, but it still dissolves right in front of you. And you spend your every waking moment trying to recapture what you had for a second, and no one else can even stand to be around you, because your obsession would drive them as mad as it's already driven you.

*

I keep looking at this picture of you in your blue sweatshirt, and it makes my heart hurt almost beyond endurance. Lorri, I love you so much that it's killing me. It hurts. I just love you, and I know that other people love you, and I hate them for it. I despise them for it. I love you, Lorri, and it's a fire in me. I need you inside me.

*

I've made progress even now. When you return, I will be better for you. I love you, Lorri. Please feel it. I love you so much.

*

I love you, Lorri. Please hurry back. I cannot live without you. I love you so much.

I am yours for eternity,

D.

March 9, 1998

My beautiful Damien,

Mara just called to tell me she got an email from Grove Pashley
that [WM3.org] are running a full-page ad in the *Arkansas Times* of
you in the April 24th issue and they are trying to get as many people
as possible to go to your hearing. This is going to be all of that stuff,
isn't it? The press, a lot of people. It doesn't even bother me—I will
just sit off by myself and no one will even know I'm there but you.
Do you think there is any way Ron can get them to let you be with
me? Even to touch you for a moment? Will you be able to wear
street clothes?

I just started thinking about all of that. It doesn't even make me
feel strange, just like I am your wife and we'll do what has to be
done. My presence there will calm you. All you will have to do is
look at me and you will be fine, because you looking at me will do
that to me. We will be the only ones in the room, so I'm OK. I know
we will be able to do this and it will be just fine. There is no reason
for you to ever worry about me. For this is what I am here for, my
love, to be with you—no matter how crazy or insane it gets.

That's how it is supposed to be, that is why we are the way we
are together—to get through this stuff—well, I should say that's
about 1 in a trillion reasons why.

Your love,

Lorri

March 11, 1998

Beautiful one,

My love, we cannot be upset about the court thing. It will be over
before you know it. It doesn't even matter. Lorri, you have to be
strong for me. This is going to be hard enough for me as it is; I could
not even begin to deal with it if you start that business again. I swear
that I won't even try. They will have to feed me, put my clothes on
for me, carry me into the courtroom, and sit me in the chair,
because I will refuse to do anything myself. I will just sit there and
stare into space. But if you hold up, then we will walk through it
without even thinking of it, without even paying attention to it.
Maybe we'll even have a little fun. And I must say that it is going to
be fun to wear something that you pick out. You probably shouldn't
get a tie though, I probably couldn't have it. They're paranoid. And
yes, I will try again to get to touch you. I will try my damndest.

I feel so naked without my hair. Like a turtle that has been
stripped of its shell. It feels awful. When we are together, there will
never be another haircut. I must admit that there are certain
advantages though. I don't have to brush it. It only takes a minute to
wash it, and it doesn't get in the way while exercising. Still, I would
never do it by choice.

There's a ghost in my head tonight, love. I'm just glad it's not in
my heart.

There's a song about you by a man named Al Stewart. It's called "Year of the Cat." Never has another song been so much about you. Now the ghost is in my heart.

I am yours for eternity,

D.

April 11, 1998

My beautiful Damien,

I forgot to tell you, when I came to see you on Thursday, one of the guys working out front said, "Mz. Echols, right?"

I love that.

And I love you.

And I will forever.

Lorri

April 17, 1998

My love,

   This week was horrible—but I did learn something . . . or I
realized something. If we are unhappy or arguing about
something . . . we will not ever go to bed without making it all right,
without bringing each other back to our place. The only safe place
that exists. The only place I want to exist.

   So I will never, ever be sad that you haven't called. I'll just know
you can't.

   And yes, I grind my own coffee and you've been listening to too
many country songs—Damien, it's the only kind of coffee to drink!

                              I love you, my dear, forever,

                                                  L.

April 29, 1998

My Beautiful Love,

The anticipation of this court hearing is wearing down my
nerves. I don't want to do this. Last time it was horrible, but this
time will be even worse. And they say it lasts all day long. That is
better than I had first expected, because I thought it would last two
or three days. At least it will not be so long. But that does not make
me look forward to it any more. And I do know that everything is
going to be just fine, so don't you start up with your business. I
know it will all be fine, and all I have to do is look at you, but that
does not make me like it any better. Everything is as it's meant to
be. Ka.

I feel so much different this night than I did last night. It is
amazing, these extremes that you take me to, you magickal creature.
I feel very happy and close to you now. Earlier, before we talked, I
felt so irritated, but once you made me start to giggle, I found even
my own irritation to be humorous. I love you so much. You are pure
magick, like a beautiful little unicorn.

Love, this hair business is driving me insane. It's almost to the
point of wanting to claw it off. It will be a huge relief to just get rid
of it all and start over. And then it will grow back even thicker,
darker, and more beautiful than even before. It will just take a few
months, but you will be pleased with the end result. I would like to

get it done before that photographer gets here, because I want to get copies of the pictures for you, and I would like you to have pictures of the two extremes—long hair and no hair.

I am yours for eternity, beautiful one,

D.

May 6, 1998

My Beautiful One:

Damien . . . everything about the last two days—I feel I have
either learned so much, or it has just been confirmed in me—things
I have always known. I am so in love with you and before I can write
anything else . . . I am completely intoxicated by your smell—I
waited an hour for those clothes—but I would've waited forever—
they smell like you and it's the smell I know so well now—it makes
me crazy—it makes me want you so badly. Even when I'm sitting in
that stupid courtroom . . . I look at you and feel everything fall out
of me and I feel that oh-so-familiar feeling that only you can make
happen. But when you stood up—near the end and I was looking at
you—when you first stood up I felt I was going to faint—I have
never seen you like that—in those kinds of clothes, with a belt (!),
but just seeing you standing there, looking at me—every time I
think of it I can't breathe. You are so incredible, Damien, you are so
beautiful and you are so poised and graceful and dignified—even
around all of those idiots and it is so apparent. I look at you and I
feel so proud and I feel that I want to hold you so close. Being in that
room with all of those people, I still felt it was just us. There is no
one else. I feel it so much right now. I can't even begin to tell you
and I am exhausted—

But I want to tell you so much more. Tomorrow. And I am going
crazy to talk to you.

I'm going to sleep, my love.

Your mom hugged me. And I want to tell you things Ron said. Sweet.

Damien, I am at work, now, and I am almost ready to die, it feels—but it's wonderful. I love you so much and I miss you so much. I didn't realize what the repercussions would be from spending a whole day in the same room with you, looking at you—I only know that my whole body hurts with wanting you.

I saved your letters to read this morning—and I sat here crying when I read the letter you wrote on Sunday—I have so much to say about it, Damien, I will bring the two parts of you together—and you aren't becoming like me—we are becoming one thing. We have always been heading towards that. Yesterday, when I was looking at you—I would at times be so overcome with what you are to me. I am looking at my entire life—right there before me is everything. And no one even knows how much is between you and me and I am so happy for that—and you made me so proud and you made me so strong.

What I was going to tell you about Ron—when he first got there, I think he felt strange and I was sitting by myself (as I wanted) and then Ron asked if he could sit by me—which seemed somehow right. Later on he said the reporters asked him who I was . . . was I "Damien's girlfriend" and Ron said "no"—then he came over to me and said, "Lorri, they're asking about you—you shouldn't get messed up in them. I don't want them to touch you—so be careful—if anyone asks, you work for me."

So I just stayed in the courtroom the whole time . . . Damien, I got there at 7:30!! And I stayed through lunch except to make a call to Susan and except for that one recess when I went to get an apple because I hadn't eaten since noon on Monday. At that point Ron stopped me outside. I thanked him for being so kind to me and he said, "Lorri, I just want to thank you for what you've become to

Damien, living the way you two do, your life together, it has to be very strong, very special—if you ever need anything you call me because I love Damien to death"—I couldn't take it anymore and then I had to go to the bathroom and sob. But it wasn't sad. It was a relief. Then I came back upstairs and it seemed I had been gone for hours. I cannot stop thinking of how beautiful you were standing there—you had to roll up the pants?! Those little legs of yours. Maybe I should get more pants for the next time. In another shade of gray perhaps? (Not that I have a whole lot to work with!)

Something changed in me yesterday. Something very, very deep and important. The only thing that matters is you. And getting you with me. And I know it's going to happen. But it's a feeling of strength. And fearlessness and even a place that no one can touch. We are above it all, yet we are right there in it . . . and I can do *anything*. I know I can—with you. We both can, and we will. Damien, I didn't even mind any of it, it just felt like another place with you, and everything swirls around us. I love you so much—and yes—everything would be better if we were together, but the thing is—even though we're not yet—look at what we've done.

You have a sweetness in you that I cannot begin to explain—but it is so pure and I can see it and I feel it. It is the color of honey and when light touches it, it is gold and dazzling—but when it is in the shadow you cannot even see the depth of it. This is what I feel. Damien, I exist only to love you. And I know I will be here for a long, long time because of you.

Damien, I love you more than I could ever say and I feel more a part of you than I ever have.

Soon, I will have you, I can feel it.

I am so in love with you.

Lorri

May 9, 1998

My Damien,

Congratulations! Our phone bill was only $500! It's an improvement! And that included other calls, $90. So ours was $410!! Oh, I hope that other number works! We will soon know.*

Your beloved,

Lorri

---

* I set up a virtual phone at one point—there was a company that figured out that a local call from the prison had a surcharge and then a horrific minute-by-minute charge; there was no "local call." So this company set up a local phone number for a customer to be forwarded from the prison—a middleman, essentially. I cut out the middleman, setting up a virtual local phone number in Tucker, Arkansas, so Damien would call, and the call would be forwarded to me, then my cell phone. Eventually the prison found out—I told a few other people about it, who had set up their own local numbers, too—and threatened to take my phone number off the list completely so Damien wouldn't be able to call. At that point I had multiple numbers, so that if one was shut off, we'd try another—it was a miracle when call forwarding to my cell phone came along—I was no longer stranded, and Damien could reach me anywhere.—LD

June 2, 1998

My love,

   They will probably be here to pick me up for court one week
from today. I'm not even "fretting" over it anymore. It will be
nothing. Except I get to see you for two days!!

                                    *

Love, this part of Arkansas is nothing like West Memphis.
Everything is different. They don't even have winter here. If you
remember, last year they had 3 feet of snow in Memphis and W.
Memphis, yet there was not even so much as a single flake here. The
entire feel is different. Everything here is base, disgusting, pathetic.
Nothing of me.

                                         I belong to you,

                                                D.

August 3, 1998

My Damien:

   Today was sublime. The last two messages you left for me—how painful it was not to answer the call—both times it hurt so badly, for all I want is you. When you said, "This is the last message, love," I felt my knees go weak. You are so, so romantic and you make me so happy—I want so much to be with you, to touch you, to make love with you. I want so much to have your child, to wake up with you every morning or every night. You fill my thoughts constantly. You are my everything and yes, my love, this weekend was wonderful with you.

*

Maybe with the letter thing, occasionally you send me one or some. You don't have to send me all of them, or read all of them, just some of them. So at least I will know what is coming in the mail from you. I do want to know these things, Damien, and I'll behave myself. What is her name again, the one who lives in Michigan? Do you write back to her most of the time? Does the other one write?

   It was nice of her to offer those books to you. You seem to like the books they send you, you've read a lot of them.

   I should leave you alone about them, because it seems they really do care for you and are devoted in some way and you have built a relationship with them and I should be supportive of it. So I will. One of their names is Helen, right? It seems they had kind of old-fashioned names.

I really am trying, my love. I don't want to cause you any distress (unnecessary distress).

*

I ordered *Lolita* for you from the bookstore and I asked the woman who took my order if she needed me to spell your name and she said, "No, I know how to spell his name." I almost hung up on her. The fact that she even said "his name" was enough to send me over the edge. And I hate to admit this, my lover, but it makes me jealous that you are going to read that book. Even though I read it, still, it's going to make me jealous.

*

I am having one of those times when I can feel you so close and I know I will have you with me. Damien—you will be with me. All we have to do is be patient. But on a day like today, it's the hardest thing in the world to ask of me, because I need you so badly. I need your body and your breath and your touch, I need to feel you take me completely—just hold me, make love to me until I have not an ounce of energy left and then don't even stop. Crumble me up in a small round thing and hold me until I can't breathe. Pull my hair and hold my hands and put yourself into every part of me so you mark me as yours.

I love you, Damien. It hurts, but it's exquisite.

L.

August 3, 1998

My lover,

I cannot wait to get all of those college books. I feel as if I am undertaking a huge task. I'm very excited about it, too. By the time I do get to school, I won't even have to open a single book. I'll finish all my work in a matter of minutes, make perfect grades, and have plenty of time to look around and examine everyone and everything else. I cannot stop thinking about those books. I can hardly wait for this.

*

You'll not be getting any of those letters that people send, because when I sent them to you a long time ago, it hurt you very badly, and you made me promise that I would look out for you, and not let you have anything that would harm you, no matter how hard you begged. You made me promise you that. So I cannot let you have them. I'm just looking out for your best interests, and my sanity.

*

I do not understand why you say you liked New York so much, if it's as disgusting as you say. But I cannot wait to go there with you. I think of going places with you all the time now. I want to go everywhere with you and do everything with your beautiful little self.

*

I just watched a National Geographic show about sperm whales. Lorri, I cannot get in the ocean. It terrifies me. It's a nightmare. It's not even the creatures I'm thinking of, it's all that water. I would lose my mind in it, I would not be able to stop screaming. I can't do it, Lorri, I'm just too scared. I don't want you trying to make me do it, either. There are things in there, Lorri. I can feel them. I can't even look at pictures of it without getting chills, and my stomach feels like it's falling. I can handle a swimming pool, and the river won't bother me. I don't know about a lake. It depends on what it looks like. In my dreams I'm always flying, and it seems to be the most natural thing in the world, I don't even think about it. And I would love to be fire. I would swim in it. But I cannot take the big waters.

I love you,

D.

August 4, 1998

My beloved:

I know when I am so intensely sad at being apart from you, I know it makes it very hard on you—but there are times in this life with you that it becomes . . . not unbearable, for it is a pain I accept—it is almost "home" to me or at least it is something I understand completely—but I want to be happy for all of this love I feel—not sad.

But it is during these times when it is so intense that I feel myself falling deeper—it's been like this for a while and I love it—oh, I love you more, more with each passing minute, but these passages of time that I feel myself in at the moment . . .

It is like falling down a very, very long flight of stone steps—it hurts so much, but not enough to kill me, or even scar me, yet I want to keep falling for it is taking me to a much deeper place in the house—that's just what it seems like. My love for you has always been this way, it affects me physically—it manifests itself in my body—as well as my heart and soul. I wish you could feel how strong it is within me—how it will accomplish what it needs to bring you to me.

Today, when I was walking from my car to my house, a voice sprung out of nowhere, it was kind of amused, but it said, "Aren't you amazed at how fast everything is happening—you are now living in Arkansas and you were sent here to receive him!" That's what I mean—the magick is very strong now, I can feel it—the magick that has brought us together.

*

Did you watch *Rebecca*? I am trying to listen or watch every little thing that you do, even more than ever—'cause it does something to me—but sometimes watching TV hurts too much. I don't want you to see that stuff. I know that sounds awful. But I don't. I don't want you to see any of it. I'm in a very, very possessive way right now . . . And yet, none of it can touch you or touch me.

Yours forever,

L.

August 6, 1998

My Dearest One,

I feel a little hurt tonight, wounded. It's because I keep thinking
of the things you were saying, about how you feel alone, because
you are going through something right now that is not the same as I
feel. And you say, "You sound good," as if it's an accusation. It
makes me feel as if I am the one who is alone. You always act as if
you are the only one who ever has to feel some things, as if I am
completely exempt from any suffering or pain. Well, I am not. And it
makes me feel as if the things I say to you never penetrate very
deeply, they only float on the surface. Or maybe only select things.
You seem to pick the things you want to penetrate and those you do
not. I say that because I've told you a thousand times before when I
was feeling as you now are. Yet now you still feel as if you're the
only one. I'm really, really trying not to sound bitter or mean,
because I know it's just my hurt feelings that are talking right now.
I'll deal with it and all will be well.

All day long I kept thinking about how I know exactly how you
are feeling, so I must be so, so sweet with you, and handle you so
gently. I must be whispers and rose petals. Yet, now I feel very
selfish, as if I am making things even harder for you.

I really wish I could carry you through this time, love. I would
take it all for you if I could. I would make sure you never felt any

pain. I love you so much, Lorri. I hope you can feel that. One day I'll find a way to show you. I love you, I love you, I love you. We'll be together soon. I belong to you.

I am yours for eternity,

D.

September 1, 1998

My dearest:

I'm having one of those days when I am overcome with the love I have for you, and the love you have for me—it is euphoria, Damien, it is why I live.

Tonight, I leave to come see you. Well, to come look at you for 3 days—to be near you while they hold you in that place—but I'll be holding you so close to me. I know you will feel it the whole time.

Yes, we will have fun this time and I will not shed a tear—there is no reason for me to be sad—my heart skips a beat just thinking of being in the same room with you with no glass between us—just wood, chairs, and bodies—much easier than ¼″ glass.

Damien, that Sarah that works at the prison—who takes my appointments to see you—she's good—she always wants me to see you—I called her today and thanked her for it. I don't do things like that often—but I did today. I hope she stays there for a while.

I am amazingly calm—I hope you are as well. I look forward even to the nights of just sitting in that hotel room alone—feeling you. It reminds me of when I used to come down here to see you. How I would sit in those unknown places—yet I knew you were so close by.

I never want you to be physically separated from me again. I will always go where you go. I feel better than I ever have about one of these things. Very strong, very confident. Something is going to happen, I can feel it, yet I protect that feeling—not to "jinx" it so to speak. It's good.

You have a whole wardrobe to choose from this time. I hope the stuff is OK.

You'll be lovely.

I must leave. I love you, Damien.

Lorri

October 9, 1998

My love,

The court date draws near. This time I look forward to it. It even
excites me to know I will soon be wearing the clothes you have
chosen for me.

It's almost Samhain, All Hallow's Eve, Halloween. It will be a
good one this year. No pain, only fun.

Do you know that it used to be customary to pay the executioner
that would behead you? That way he would do it in one stroke and
get it over with, because sometimes it would take him four or five
tries to do it correctly. And if there were many to be killed on the
same day, everyone wanted to be the first, so that the blade was still
sharp. Then a French doctor invented the guillotine.

Forever,

D.

October 13, 1998

My Dearest:

  Today at breakfast I thought, "I need advice." I haven't asked
advice, except from you, in so, so long—and I thought . . . who is the
wisest person I know? And my first thought was you!! But I can't ask
you advice about this. If I am quiet enough and don't let myself get
all riled up and I stay out of it and just trust you to do whatever you
have to do—then isn't that the best advice? Look within my own
heart for the answer?

I love you, Damien,

Lorri

October 26, 1998

My Dearest:

Here I sit in this courtroom—Damien, you look so incredibly beautiful. You really are perfection. It looks like they let you have the brush; I can't tell about the razor. I'm not so freaked out about all of these people. It feels good, all I feel is how much I love you, how much I adore you.

I am unable to see the shoes—your mom came up to me and said to tell you that you look so beautiful in your glasses. And she's going to be here all week. Melissa* asked a bailiff if I could come up and see you, but he said no. She said she would keep checking.

*

Cally called right before I left on Sunday to wish you much luck, as did Susan. You are much loved my dear, and that is a good thing, because what's not to love?

Eat, Damien, whatever it is—meat, bread, milk, I don't care—eat enough. I asked Cally to call Ed Mallett to ask him to take those chains off. It doesn't look like she was successful.

Melissa said she is happy to be here for you, she likes talking to

---

* Melissa was a colleague of Damien's lead counsel, Ed Mallett, at the time. Cally is a dear friend and, officially speaking, Damien's adoptive mother, who had been writing letters to Damien from nearly the beginning of his incarceration. She and her husband, Douglas, funded Damien's entire Rule 37 appeal.—LD

you. That makes me happy, too. It's going well, my love, even
Melissa said so, and she isn't usually very forthcoming with hope.

*

I am staying at the Wilson Inn. It's better than the last place I stayed
and not nearly as bad as where you are staying.

*

I swear when you walked into the courtroom there was an audible
gasp from the crowd—probably because you look so fetching.

I love you, my dear, and I am with you forever,

L.

October 27, 1998

Damien,

I am going to try something, I am going to make this happen. At the next recess I am going to approach the bailiff myself and if he wants to lord over us, I don't care. I will try with each and every bailiff until someone lets me come up there.

I like this forensic odontologist—he reminds me of a Dr. Seuss creature.

I find myself feeling faint, especially today because I am so close to you. After that Branch man* caused his disturbance, I felt all of the blood drain from my face and I felt myself faint for just a second. They are pulling out your dental casts now.

I wonder if this exhausts you—it must, it exhausts me. It must be 100 times worse for you.

I am with you eternally,

L.

---

* The father of one of the victims rushed the bench during Damien's Rule 37 hearing. He was restrained and quickly escorted out of the courtroom.—LD

November 2, 1998

My Beautiful One,

I had to borrow an envelope, because I could not stand the thought of one more day and you not getting a letter from me.

Lorri, nothing will ever be the same again. I still cannot completely absorb the fact that we have actually touched. I have pressed my lips to your beautiful hand. It is something that must filter in slowly. I have not stopped thinking about it since that very moment. Does it not seem like a miracle to you? We have touched. And it was the most natural thing I have ever felt. That was the touch I was created to feel. Experiencing that touch is the reason I exist. And now I miss you a billion times more than I ever have before. I must be with you soon, or the strain will rip me apart. My need for you is so great.

Yes, Love, I want to be married to you now. I want it so badly. I want you to be my wife. It's just one more step in our process, but it's a wonderful and magickal step. The only thing that makes me sad is the fact that I cannot get you a wedding ring. Thinking of it hurts me, because you have to have one. I want to be married to you, my beautiful creature. As soon as possible. It's exciting just to think about.

*

Before you found me, I was planning on going back to the hospital when I was released from here. And I would have probably stayed there forever. You are all that I want, need, and desire. My love.

Your loving husband,

D.

November 12, 1998

My Love,

   I am now watching this show on Frank Lloyd Wright. It has done something to me. It has given me a better understanding of what you do and why you are so proud of it. And I am immensely proud of you. But I'm also very jealous. I'm jealous because you are so proud of your work, and because it means so much to you. It hurts me a little (a lot right now) and I am jealous because I don't want you to be proud of or care about anything but me.

   Even tonight, when you spoke of the map you are drawing for that book. Of course I am proud of that, knowing that your work was published in a book, that many, many people will see it. But I am also jealous, because I want no one else to ever look at anything you touch. I am proud of you. More so than you know.

I am yours for eternity,

D.

November 24, 1998

My loved one,

I got the phone bill . . . $558.00—a little better! I think we should strive for $400.00 or $350—then we can get married faster! I think we can do it—don't you??

Forever yours,

L.

November 30, 1998

My dearest,

I'm going to see an apartment tomorrow in the "good" neighborhood. It's a little more expensive than mine now. That hurts a bit. Well, I'll see what happens. The more I think, the more I want to stay put—but you never know what may come along when you least expect it, Mr. Man.

I love you forever,

L.

March 22, 1999

My beautiful one,

My father called—my parents are coming on Thursday! They are staying the weekend. By the time they leave they will know all about you. I find the more people that know, the better it is. As a matter of fact, I love it.

After we are married, I am going to become a lot more adamant about being kept apprised of anything that concerns you. I really will be a Yoko Ono. I am also going to post a message on that email list thanking people on your behalf for coming out to support you—is that OK?

And I love the fact that I "marked" you—but you marked me, too.

Mara says she wants to have dinner with my parents so she can help explain everything about your case—and so they won't think I've gone insane or something—no reflection on you, my darling—it's the circumstances.

Forever yours, your betrothed,

L.

postscript, 2014

I didn't even tell my family about my relationship with Damien until 1999, a few months before we were married. By that time, the case was becoming known in the media with the help of *Paradise Lost*, and I had begun to take a lead in the formation of a legal strategy for the case. Before I told my family, I felt I wanted to have a plan, I wanted to have my life appear to be worked out, as if I were building a career and making sound decisions. Even though I felt I was moving ahead instinctually, and I was living the life I wanted to live, with no questions, I didn't realize it wouldn't ever look like that to anyone else. At least not at that point. Most people came around later.

I'll never forget the day I told my parents about Damien. My father's face looked as if it had folded in on itself. He couldn't look at me; but looking back, I think he was more confused than anything. The shock that hit both of them, it was as if they were deer, and the hunter's spotlight had suddenly shone in their eyes, temporarily blinding them. I didn't know how to make it any easier for them, either. That Damien was innocent, that he didn't belong there—none of it got through.

Years later, Damien still in prison, as I was taking a walk with my mom, she told me how very sad she was for me, that I was alone, that I was still living alone. I'll never know if she understood me when I tried to explain to her that I was never alone. Having Damien in my life was like having him live inside me, that's how close we were. However, overall my parents couldn't have been more supportive, loving, and concerned—for both Damien and me. After their first visit with him, they considered Damien family and have never wavered.

Of course, I couldn't leave anything to routine when it came to Damien's well-being, and that included the prison. I began to devise schemes for getting food to him, or treats, or simple health care items like dental floss. It all made Damien very nervous; if we were caught it would mean my visits would be suspended for a year.

I was not daunted. At one point I tied a string that was fastened to a piece of fabric filled with fruit to the crotch of my underwear. I put on a long, very full skirt over it and practiced walking, the parcel of fruit swinging between my knees like a pendulum. I had to practice so my gait wouldn't look weird. On Damien's birthday, December 11, I wore a thick cable-knit sweater over a bra that contained a piece of homemade devil's food cake in each cup.

I tried to dress in a way that would make Damien happy. I wasn't much of a fashion plate in my day-to-day life, but I grew to love changing into a southern Holly Golightly for my weekly visits to Tucker

Max. I wore pencil skirts with four-inch heels and stockings and I'd have my hair done. I'd wear makeup as I never had before: eyeliner, polished nails. It was all very girly and fun. I'd never felt like that before, and I give Damien all the credit.

Lorri

March 29, 1999

My love,

Beautiful one, I love that your parents know now. It surpassed everything I imagined. It makes everything feel different. I like the questions they ask. I'm so happy, Lorri. Now I want your sisters to know. And I want to go to one of those family reunions with your sexy self. I love you so, so much. I can't stop thinking about them knowing, how happy it makes me. You have made me so proud, Lorri. You truly never cease to amaze me.

I love you,

D.

April 1999

My lovely one,

    Lorri, I love how your family has responded. I cannot even describe how much it means to me. Every time you begin to talk about it, my heart starts to flutter. They're so sweet, your mother carrying those books around, and your sister asking if you sent "naked pictures" because I need them. And saving those baby clothes. I love it. Tomorrow, I am going to have to get every tiny detail out of you.

I love you,

Damien

April 27, 1999

My beautiful one,

I want to know what my sister wrote to you. She may need some censoring. She might be telling things she doesn't know anything about. I know she is going to tell you the bird in the closet story. There are so many things we did when we were little with my older sister—Gee Man and Bea and Martha (my older sister was the dad—Gee Man was my older sister, too, although Gee Man had many personalities including Buzz Horse, Fat Pup, the list goes on and on). Young and I would have to respond to each of these people. Sometimes death would be involved. There are a myriad of stories like this. It seems we constantly lived in a fantasy world.

I like that she wrote you, though. My whole family is going to just love you. Even my grandmother, Dolls. She calls black people "gumdrops" or "jiggaboos." Her birthday was yesterday and as usual, I forgot. I'm already on her blacklist.

Forever yours,

L.

April 28, 1999

My love,

I am extremely pleased to have gotten this letter from your sister.
I will send it to you as soon as I have responded to it. You leave her
alone about those stories, because I'll have them. She said you
warned her not to. I demand that you leave her be. I'm very excited
about writing to her.

And yes, sweet, grubby little thing, I am very excited about being
married to you. I can't wait for it. Once you put that ring on my
hand, I will never, ever take it back off. I want to be married to you.
It gives me butterflies in my stomach.

I love you, sweetness,

D.

May 19, 1999

My beautiful Damien,

By the by, I looked up that guy who asked me to go hiking in the phone book—no! not "hiking in the phone book"—I looked up his name in the phone book, I called him and told him why I didn't want to go hiking with him, lest he thought I was being coy—he laughed and said he appreciated the call—then he said—well, he can go hiking, too!! And I said, well, not at the moment, no, and if he doesn't go, I don't go. I'm glad I did it, it felt good. Things should be clear—it feels better when they are—just like when I told my parents about us. It just feels better.

And Damien, I really do want to know about all of the people who write or send gifts. I promise I'll remember to tell you of any "incidents" that I have. It really doesn't happen often; most of the men think I'm "off-limits" or something, or I don't "fit right"—even the "hike guy" was from upstate New York. At least I don't have shrines on the Internet!

I love you,

Lorri

May 25, 1999

My lovely one,

    I am really excited about doing the second half of *Paradise Lost*. This is my chance to talk about you. This will be perfect. This will be as it should be. You must talk to Bruce and Joe about sneaking in with them. It would be easy.

I love you,

D.

May 26, 1999

My beautiful Damien,

   Bruce and Joe called me today. They asked about the wedding, offered their congratulations (civilized people, at last). They asked if they could film it! I didn't even hesitate and I'm sorry, my love, for not consulting you first, but I said "no." They said, "Somehow we are not surprised you said that!" Then they asked if I wanted to come down for the filming and I said, "Yes, of course." They said they are coming the second week of June.
   I get nervous when I think of it, but I am excited for you.

Forever yours,

Lorri

June 2, 1999

My Lorri,

   I didn't get a letter from you today. I got one from everyone in the world, except for you. I will have one tomorrow, I know. And so will you. And then I see you in just one day.

                              I am yours forever,

                                        D.

June 18, 1999

My beautiful Damien:

I have been thinking all evening how after we were talking about the judge's decision and all . . . and you said, "I guess it's not time for me to come out of here yet." (I'm sure I didn't phrase that correctly). You make me want to cry sometimes. I love you so much—I hurt tonight, I am in physical pain because of you.

I love you beyond measure,

Lorri

June 1999

My Dearest,

Reading [*Blood of Innocents*] made me think about something.
Damien, it's horrible the way they write about you, attaching your
thoughts to the character in that book. There was the part about
your physical attractiveness to women, there was a part where it
says, "You began to realize the attractiveness of your sister." That
was very strange. It's such a weird little blot.

But there were definitely parts that I recognized. Things you said
that were a part of your mental health records—the part when you
went to the hospital—and began to feel comfortable there . . . I
know all of that. So it was strange coming across things that were
familiar and things that were completely foreign to me.

*

At night, when I am lying in my bed, I like to look over at you next
to me. I always talk to you—I used to just send my words out into
the night—the color of it was always the same—but now I see you
next to me. It has changed. I do it every night. We can talk about
anything, and that's exactly how it is . . . we just start talking.
Sometimes the light is on and I can see you plainly. Other times, I
wait til all the lights are out—'cause I like to think of being with you
in bed when all of the lights are out.

*

When we are married, we can have a joint bank account! I like to
think of those things. Damien, there is so much I want to do with

you. So very, very much. And don't you be snarling at the thought of having a bank account. It can actually work very well. We'll have no keeping our money in a jar out in the yard.

*

Damien, I want to send a gift to Seth—can we do that? I want him to know us, I would love to have him come stay with me. I would do all kinds of things with him. I'd bring him with me to come visit you—I'd make food for him.

I love you, beautiful one,

L.

July 27, 1999

My lovely,

Sometimes, I wonder what things must be like out there for you. It must be so different than in here. I can't even begin to imagine it. It's too alien to me.

*

Lorri, I learn more every day. The point is not to feel nothing. The point is to feel everything. When I am angry, I must become the anger. I must erase any dividing line between myself and the anger. That's the way. You have to monitor your every thought, and realize that that's exactly what they are—only thoughts, not the truth. We fight because we both think our thoughts are the truth. The goal is not to stop thinking, but realize exactly what we are thinking, and realize that we are indeed thinking. That is enlightenment. No one can always do it, but the more we practice, the more we can do it. There's a huge difference between someone that does it most of the time and someone who hardly does it at all.

   Another thing is that the reason we get into any type of relationship is because of selfishness—we want something from it. That's not bad. That's OK. When the other person in the relationship doesn't do or give us exactly what we want, we get angry or sad, and try to change them. Like when people say they need to "learn to communicate better." What they mean is, "I want you to understand what I want from you." It's OK to realize that no one can ever always do what we want 100% of the time. See, that's why you get upset when I say to you that "I can't" do something. That's the last thing you want to hear, because it tells you that you won't always get what you want. And you were right. Because I do act like a baby when you show weakness, because it's not what I want. I always want you to be so strong, above everything, where nothing but me can touch you. Then when I hear you cry about something else, my feelings get hurt. And why do my feelings get hurt? Because I don't get exactly what I want. Lorri, the key is practice. We have to pay attention to our thoughts. There's no magick cure to fix everything up. It takes time and practice. And I am willing. Hell, I have no choice.

I am yours,

Damien

August 6, 1999

Damien,

I was thinking about the top 5 reasons why you are still a baby.
There are many reasons—but these are the top 5. They may change
daily—but some of them include:

1. You still watch *Spider-Man*
2. You eat a medley of salty treats for dinner

There are more, but not right now.

3. You still get carsick
4. You cry at *Montel Williams*

Damien! You are so sweet. And yet you speak all day in the
nastiest way—even more than Gene Perry! I know you're capable of
it, too. It's nastiness. I would give anything to be able to listen to you
all day without you knowing it. I'm not surprised at all, I know you
have that part of you—it's the nasty side of you. It is very much a
part of you. And like everything else, I am very, very attracted to
it—because I want to know what is all there. Where it comes from,
and I want to hear what all of those guys get to hear every day. No
matter how nasty it is.

Love,

L.

August 19, 1999

My lovely one,

You may have to call this chaplain, because I didn't know your work phone number. I gave them the home number, so he'll be calling on my phone line. I feel like we're so much closer to being married now. It became a lot more concrete for me today, filling out those papers. We're going to be married! It's going to put a little more of a barrier between us and everything else. I'm so in love with you, my beautiful one. I want to wear a ring that you put on my hand. Once you slide it on my finger, I will never, ever take it off again. It will be the mark for the world to see that I belong to you. You'll have to make a copy of that wedding license for me, so I can look at it all the time. You have to put the real one in a frame and hang it in the living room, so that everyone who walks in the door will see it. You will be my wife, you beautiful little animal.

                                        I love you,

                                        Damien

October 18, 1999

My dearest,

Well my dear, what I have really not wanted to ever do—is going to have to be done. I'm going to have to ask for money—borrow money from someone—the question is—who? I cannot survive anymore on what I have and I don't want my credit to be ruined—if we ever wanted to buy a house or anything, we wouldn't be able to—I can't even pay my bills anymore. It really is that bad and I have to face up to it. Depending on how the phone bill comes in, we may have to cut back even more. I need to keep the phone bill at $400, as opposed to $700 or $800.

I know it sounds awful, but we just have to do it and I have to come to terms with what my life is turning into—I don't want to be constantly worrying about money, it's not good—and instead of complaining about it, we fix it. That's all.

Actually, who I should ask for money is David—he owes me money from when we were together. He'll give it to me, too. I don't want to ask my parents—or Linda and Mara—actually, I could ask Lucy—she would help!

I've been very, very foolish. But I still don't regret a minute I've ever spent on the phone with you. And it's not that bad—I just can't finagle my way out of it any longer. I feel better already, just accepting it. I can pay it all back within the year.

And then, maybe we'll get the money from Bruce and Joe—you should call Ed Mallett and ask about that this week.

I love you, beautiful,

L.

November 12, 1999

My dearest:

I had the strangest dreams all night. I dreamed I was put into prison and I was so scared, because I didn't know how I was going to talk to you. They took away my clothes and made me wear a big baggy dress and they cut all of my hair off. I somehow kept a dress of my own with me and put it on at one point—but was scared of what they would do to me. The food was good, though—they had a wonderful apple pie. The main thing was the separation from you. It was unbearable—then I got a letter!! And it was the same mail lady as you have there.

That dream lasted all night! Even when I would wake from it, it would resume.

Forever,

L.

December 6, 1999

My Love,

I am still in awe of the fact that we are now actually married. It
was the most wonderful, magickal thing I've ever experienced.
Lorri, it was a miracle how everything just happened so perfectly,
with no flaws. I never thought it would have gone so wonderfully. I
just wish that everyone could have come. Every single person at that
reception should have been there.* And they can be, when we do it
again. Lucy definitely has to do the ceremony again next time, too.
She was great. Lorri, I'm so thankful for everything that everyone
has done, the way people have gathered around and been so
supportive. This really was a perfect wedding ceremony. I cannot
stop thinking of how beautiful you were, and how happy you
looked standing there looking into my eyes. You're so perfect, my
beautiful monkey. You are the most exquisite thing. You deserve
everything, my lovely one. This marriage was the result of eons of
good karma. I want to write to everyone and tell them how
wonderful it was, and how happy I am. I can't wait to get that
portrait of you.

---

* We were only permitted to have six people, some of them witnesses, attend our
wedding in the prison. It was terribly hard to decide who to invite, although the reception afterward at a friend's house was attended by everyone we knew and had
become a part of our circle. I was excluded from the celebration, of course; while our
friends and family toasted our union—and the love of my life—I sat alone in a
prison cell.—DE

I loved your wedding dress, beautiful one. It was so perfect, so beautiful. There's nothing in the world more beautiful than you, or that can even come close to comparing. You are my heart, my life, and my love. You are my world. I cannot stop looking at my wedding ring, playing with it. I've already written to Randi, and told her about it, how you inscribed "To my beloved" in it. Lorri, that makes my heart soar.

I'm glad that Shelley was able to be there, because she works with you every day. That way you two can still talk about it at work. That's the greatest thing. I want you to be able to talk about it every day. Lover, it would have broken my heart if you wouldn't have had that reception, all those people around you. I'm so thankful for all of them. They've been great. And I'm really glad that Cally-rat was there. It would have even been nice to have Douglas there. Lorri, I really think you should have invited David to the reception. It would have been OK.

I think Julie and I may actually get along. Out of everyone that you know, I think she would be the only one that could actually become my friend, too. I just don't think that's possible with the hen club, and most likely not with Susan. I think I started to like Julie when I heard her get mad and say, "Fuck that shit."

I really wish it could have worked out so that I could've talked to Jason. That would've been so great. But I have no idea what I would have said.

I have finished my weekly push-ups now. And I'm almost through the Hank Williams book. It hurts my heart—I think I could have saved him. I even learned something I didn't know—his wife put out a couple of records, and he was friends with Jack Ruby, the guy who shot Oswald.

I can't wait to talk to you tonight, beautiful one. I can't get close enough to you. I want to hold you again. We have to get contact visits.

I love you, my wife,

Damien

December 7, 1999

My beloved Damien:

Lucy called early this morning—looks like we made the front page. Ha ha ha, I don't even care 'cause it's done and we don't have to worry about anything. Yay!!

I'm just so happy. I still am!! I always will be.

Burk sent another $75 for the phone fund. Those guys spent a lot of money. I sent him a note.

I'm also sending a letter from Cally that made me laugh so much.

*

People on the website are going wild about the article in the paper. It's quite a bit of fodder for them.

I love you, beautiful. I miss you so much. Everyone keeps asking how you are doing and I say he's happy just like me.

Don't you feel calm? I do.

*

Damien, you have made me so very happy. Soon you will be with me. I can feel it.

I love you.

Your wife,

Lorri

December 9, 1999

My beloved,

I just had a guy come down here and harass me about marrying you. I was surprised, I just kept my calm and said, "The truth will come out."

He was a complete ass.

My supervisor Mark was completely charming and said, "John, you should show some respect."

Well, there will always be people like that, all I can do is ignore it.

I just wrote a letter to the warden thanking him and his staff.

*

The rumor mill is spinning here at work. Everyone is gossiping about us!!

Forever,

Lorri

December 22, 1999

My lovely one,

Tomorrow is the big day. It's still hard to believe that we'll get to
be together, touching, for 3 full hours. By this time tomorrow night,
we'll have already experienced it and be counting down the days
until next time. This makes it feel like tomorrow is Friday. You are
confusing my internal clock. It's just a few more hours away,
beautiful one.

I love you, my beautiful wife,

D.

December 23, 1999

My beloved Damien:

Words cannot begin to describe what I am feeling. I am joyful—I feel my whole life has suddenly been given to me. I love you so very much, the memory of your touch is sublime. Damien, you are magnificent. You are everything. You knocked on the table and said, "This is it," but I couldn't have been more in the moment. The whole time I was with you was 100 times more than seeing a movie. I've realized lately that seeing movies was for me meditation. It always has been—I would sit in the first row completely still and I would be completely in the moment the whole time the movie was on—there was nothing else in my mind other than what was before me. But being with you yesterday was "it" for me. I was just there— with you. That is all.

Oh, how I love you, how I am so completely happy. I find I cannot even tell people because it is so magickal and beautiful and it makes me value what we have a hundred times more. All the love I feel for you erases feelings of anger and pettiness—never have I been so happy. I feel I am with you. I could smell you all night. I didn't want to take a shower.

*

All in time, my sweet husband—all in time. I am so calm, yet my heart is so full—and I am thinking of you constantly.

Damien, I am not alone—ever. You are always with me. So when you think of Christmas and me being by myself—I am not by myself—it's just like any other day to me—full of love from you. I can't help it, but I find myself anxious for the next Wednesday.

I am at work, and just now getting ready to leave—I get to leave at 3:00. I can't wait to talk to you.

I love you,

Your wife—Lorri

December 29, 1999

My love,

   I got a short note from Kobutsu today. It was very short because
he was leaving to go to Trinidad. A guy there is about to be
executed, and they're going to hang him. I didn't know they still
practiced hanging as a form of execution. It's scary to think about.

                                    *

This Zen book I've been reading is very good. It has stories from all
the old masters in it—one actually chopped off one of his student's
fingers in order to help him reach satori. Another student said
something that gave me a delicious little shiver down my spine. His
master asked him, "What is Zen-mind?" And he responded by
saying, "An enormous black sphere hurtling through a moonless
night." And that is what it feels like! Then his master told him to
rephrase his answer, and he responded, "I am having noodles for
lunch." So the teacher accepted his answer as genuine. Pure Zen.

                              I love you, my beautiful one,

                                                    Damien

January 11, 2000

My Lovely,

   I think that only recently have I adapted to be able to handle the
way you can twist and turn me emotionally so fast and quickly. In
the beginning, I don't think I was equipped to handle it, which
contributed to the agony I was going through. Now you just make
me squirm, thrash, grunt, and say, "I can't take it." One minute you
will have me so in heat, throbbing, then the next second I can't stop
laughing because of monkey spit and you protecting sex with knives
and claws, turning things into "dead meat." Then you will say
something so sweet my heart feels like it will swell and burst with
love for you, and I'll just want to wrap my arms around you and not
let anything touch you. And there are a million other things—like
how I thrash when you talk about the hens, or bristle when I hear
anything from the past. And every single one of these things can
happen in a 10-minute phone call. In the beginning it was almost an
overload. Now I just go with it, loving every second of it. Lorri,
there is not another thing like you in the entire universe. I am so
blessed to have you. I can never, ever let go of you. You are
everything, beautiful one.

                                   I am yours forever,

                                        Damien

January 12, 2000

My lovely one,

I've been thinking of something, and I want to do it. I'm going to live in this cell as if it is a monastery. Every single day, I will sit 3 times, for at least 30 minutes at a time, I will go through all the daily service in the sutra book every single day—things like the chants before and after meals, every day, and do Kwan Seum Bosals every day. I want to do more. I'm going to talk to Kobutsu about it, see what he advises. Lorri, I've been thinking about my death lately. Not so much death itself, just the aftereffects and such. What I mean is, that if something were ever to happen to me, I want you to still pursue this path with unmoving, single-minded concentration. We can't ever stop. You would still be doing it for the both of us. That's all.

I have a small shrine or altar here now. I want you to know everything. On it, I have a sheet for an altar cloth, one of those fold-out Buddhas, and 3 different cards with deities on them, the sutra book, the Dhammapada, the Diamond Sutra, both of my malas, my refuge sash, and a glass of water. You must know everything I am doing.

I am yours for eternity,

Damien

January 13, 2000

My love,

   Sometimes, I wonder how you would act if you were in this situation. Like, who in here would you talk to, what you would talk about, what you would watch on TV, what you would do outside, how you would behave in court, what you would eat, what you would buy from the store. Then sometimes I try to act like you, or what I think you would do in that particular instant. I'm so very thankful that you never have or ever will have to be in a situation like this. You are far too regal, and dignified. You are so far above anything in here.

   I love you, my beautiful wife. Nothing in this world compares to your goodness.

I am yours forever,

Damien

January 18, 2000

My beloved,

Did you see the 17-year locust stamp?

Remember when I put that story under your stamps? You were just a baby, then. And you still are.

I love you,

L.

January 27, 2000

My lovely one,

I've been very lucky in my life, and I'm so thankful for you. You are my heart. Something is happening to my brain. Everyone in the world is dead and there's a crack in me. I'll never be scared or nervous to go to court again, because the person on trial does not even exist. Neither does Brent Davis, Burnett, Gitchell, Domini, those 3 boys, or Mark Byers. Everyone died a million breaths ago. Even places can die. It all only lasts for a few minutes anyway. People don't know shit. I'm not worried though.

I love you,

D.

March 2000

My dearest,

We watched the movie* last night and everyone was so shocked about how blatant it was about John Mark Byers. My mom thinks Melissa Byers committed suicide, but they all think Byers did it. They thought you were very handsome.

*

On the email list I have become "as bad as one of those women who married Ted Bundy or Ramirez." Idiots. I am going to make up a new "alias" name so I can "burn" people if I need to. Ah ha ha ha!! You leave me alone about it.

People can't be just saying things.

I love you forever,

L.

---

*   *Paradise Lost 2: Revelations*

March 15, 2000

My lovely wife,

I'm very, very curious about what everyone thinks about the movie. Especially people who had never before heard of me. They are the main ones. It's not so important for the people who already know. This month is going to be a very exciting time. I really am thankful for Bruce and Joe. They have been like greedy little angels to this case. They even helped bring you to me. I can't wait to see what happens, especially with Eddie Vedder on the case. I love the fact that he called. You better save those messages. We shall see what we shall see.*

I love you,

Damien

---

* It turned out we did see. We saw a lot from Eddie, Nicole Vandenberg, his publicist, and the entire Pearl Jam family. They played huge arena concerts, donating their incomes to the defense fund. Eddie played a private birthday party for a guy from Microsoft who in turn donated $300K. They were constantly looking for ways to help, and were always there when we needed them. When, in 2009, it made sense to put on a concert in Little Rock to raise awareness before the Supreme Court hearing, Pearl Jam donated all their time and energy and manpower to put on the show. Nicole and Ed came down to help Lorri the week before our release, and Ed's home was the first place we went afterward.—DE

March 22, 2000

My Love,

My heart hurts very much for you today. Lorri, I feel like I understood everything this morning. I know that there's no reason why you should have to suffer through any of this stuff, like people being mean to you for no reason. And now I want more than anything to protect you from everything, and to make up to you that I didn't do it from the beginning, because I didn't see what you wanted or needed. I'm so sorry, beautiful one.

There must not be many people that were talking bad about you, because almost every single letter I am getting is offering their congratulations on the wedding. I am going to give you a lot of these letters, so you can help answer them. But I don't want you to say you're me—just tell them that you're my wife, and we're doing this together because we want to thank everyone for their support, and that it means a lot to us. I try to put at least one personal thing in every letter, so they know they're not receiving the same thing as everyone else. For example, if they say they're from West Virginia, I say, "My wife grew up in WV." Just stuff like that.

I also just finished writing to my mother, and I told her what that woman did. I told her they're trying to do the same thing to you that people did to me, that you've done nothing but stand by me, and it's sad that they would claim to be trying to help, while hurting me like this.

I love you, Lorri,

D.

May 3, 2000

My Love,

I think Christina Riggs is being executed tonight. Either tonight
or tomorrow night. The first woman to be executed in Arkansas.
She's been all over the news lately. It's sad. She expects to go to some
heaven in the clouds and be with her children. Very odd. Have you
ever thought of being in a place of torment far beyond what your
mind could imagine, and being there for eternity? Has that thought
never, ever occurred to you? Even in church? Did it never cross your
mind that perhaps evil did walk the earth, "seeking to and fro for
whomever he may devour"? Tell me what you thought.

I am yours forever,

D.

May 10, 2000

My Love,

I've sent you a present. Perhaps it will arrive at the same time as this letter. If not, it may take about two days. This money is to buy a special treat for you. I mean it, Lorri, I don't want to hear anything out of you other than "Thank you, husband." It makes me incredibly happy to be able to do this. I may not be able to do it again for a long time, so please don't ruin it by throwing a fit. Perhaps you should go to a movie, or buy something to wear—a new skirt. Maybe have some ice cream, or go out to dinner. But whatever it is has to be entirely for you, just something that makes you happy. It's a present. I love you, beautiful one, have fun.

I just talked to you in Seattle. I can't believe how grumpy I was. I hope I get the chance to talk to you again tonight, so I can tell you how much I love you. I don't want you to carry the image of me being a grouch with you all night. I'm jealous of you being out and about amongst all those people. I would give anything to be with you there. But if I were with you, then you wouldn't be there.

I am yours forever,

D.

August 2, 2000

My lovely one,

Today on 105 they're talking about when the appropriate time is in a relationship to tell someone you've been in prison. Luckily, I never have to deal with that. Ha ha ha.

I am yours forever,

D.

September 7, 2000

My beloved Damien,

I know we have been horribly irresponsible with the phone—but I am feeling a bit fragile today and I would love to talk to you. Reading [*Blood of Innocents*] makes me cry a lot. Some things remind me of you, some things remind me of me—but it seems to affect me greatly.

Actually, it is making me question my own mind—I think I am relatively healthy, but it's hard to ascertain between mental illness and magick—it's amazing to me. I can tell you that I have seen "signs and symbols" throughout my life that have led me directly to you—and I completely believe that—yet, if I were to tell anyone else, they would think me psychotic. It's not a point of being careful—it's knowing the difference. I have listened to you so many times relate "memories" or states of mind to me—that I have never questioned—I completely believe they existed or do exist for you in the way you described them—it's just like me telling you that I got "directions" from movies—when I think of how that sounds, it sounds insane, but I know that it is not. I don't have the almost manic desire to see movies anymore. There was a time it was my life's work; I would pore over the papers, the *New Yorker*, anything I could find to locate the next "clue."

I know now that it was and is real. I also know it is best to keep it between you and me.

Your wife,

Lorri

postscript, 2014

As the work on the case progressed, and as I became more of a presence in Damien's affairs regarding the prison, meaning keeping him safe and alive, I often found myself drowning. Just those things alone would've caused anyone a great deal of stress, but we were also trying to keep each other happy, in spite of it all.

Instead of indulging in bonbons and taking bubble baths—what I should have been doing—I got stricter and more disciplined as the stakes got higher. I trained to be a warrior. My meals consisted of stripped-down plates of no fun. I did ashtanga yoga and swam laps every day. I was probably at my best health ever, but I felt like a machine for much of the time. I felt if I controlled my life, I could face the craziness of everything else; prison, lawyers, and fear.

This lifestyle sustained me through the years of famine, the years when everything was hard and it looked like a frozen, winter landscape all the time. But then in 2007 I met Capi Peck, who owned a restaurant and didn't believe kale and a sweet potato was a meal. I moved in with her, and things changed fast. Capi was once described as a disciplined hedonist. Everything changed.

The 2000s were the toughest, I think, in terms of working on the case, and for Damien and me personally. We would see huge, significant movement where Damien's case was concerned, with Fran Walsh and Peter Jackson coming on board in 2005 to helm the investigation, and with their support we were able to build a legal team that would surpass any ever known on a capital case. But we also had years where nothing moved, and we were worn down to mere shadows of ourselves. There were times we didn't even recognize who we were anymore. It took a toll on our relationship, and we waged wars on each other from which we are still healing.

But it was also a time of great insight and a spiritual growth that started a whole new life for both of us. Through Damien I learned that everything comes from the Divine, and there are many ways to bring those things into the material world. It was and is a fascinating way to live, and I credit Damien, and of course God, with bringing about his release.

Lorri

September 19, 2000

My love,

Tomorrow is the big day.* I can't wait to see what happens, what it involves, and everything that will be. I hope so much that the pictures get approved. I would love for you to be able to see them, and for them to have new pictures for the articles. I can't wait to read those, too. I'm very curious to know what Mara Leveritt will write about. This is just more fodder for her book. I can very easily see opening that book and reading about her lunch and phone conversations with Kobutsu. That's why she jumped at it so quickly. At any rate, it will be fun to read it. I'm also curious to see what the very first Koan he gives me will be. When you do Koans in an "official" way like this, you have to memorize every word of it, and some of them are long. In the Rinzai school, the first Koan is always one of 3—one hand clapping, original face, or Mu. For some reason I'm still a little wary of Mu. Mu is a trap on many levels. I will try to remember every single detail and tell you everything about it.

I am yours forever,

Damien

---

* This was in reference to my Jukai ordination ceremony in the Rinzai Zen tradition of Japanese Buddhism, the first step toward priesthood. I had been practicing Zen Buddhism for probably two years at that point, and this was the point at which my teacher presented me with a Koan—a puzzle that cannot be solved with a rational mind—in a ceremony conducted by two priests.—DE

September 19, 2000

My Damien:

My heart feels like it has a little hammer in it today—just pounding away—every time I think of you having your ceremony, and my eyes fill up with tears. I am so proud of you. You have come so far, my dearest one. I can't even tell you how much I love and respect you.

You will make a great teacher (you already are) but someday, you will be a great teacher, Damien. How I wish I could be with you today and share in your happiness. You know I am with you in your heart, I am with you always—but I wish I could see you while this is taking place. I'm so glad Kobutsu arranged it, I'm so happy for it. I will send him a thank-you note.

I hope it's going well. I can't believe how nervous I am. I've been like a jittery rabbit all day, or rather a jittery monkey. I hope you call as soon as it's finished!! If I don't hear from you before I go sit, it will be a very good practice.

I'm a bit melancholy today. I miss you very much. I know I'm being a baby, but tears just keep coming. I want to be with you.

From your weeping monkey-wife,

Lorri

October 17, 2000

My beloved,

   The movie went very well last night—it was packed and there
were so many questions. They had a prosecutor on the panel, and
she was just torn to shreds by the crowd—everyone kept asking her
what the evidence was against you—and she had none—eventually
she said, "It's not a perfect system," and this one guy in the audience
went wild—he was so angry—then she said, "We don't just pick
people off the street," and people were yelling at her. It was pretty
bad for her—but what does anyone expect? Anytime this comes
up—the people against you are always so stupid and the people who
are pro always sound intelligent. This prosecutor even said "ain't"
one time. You know how I feel about grammar. It was very telling.*

                                        I love you, beautiful.

                                                L.

---

* This was a screening at the Hot Springs Documentary Film Festival of *Paradise
Lost 2*, and there was a discussion panel at the end of it. I don't recall who the specific
people were on this panel, though it was entirely different from any other screenings
of the film I'd been to, because they invited people from both sides of the case to
weigh in. The room was packed and emotions were running very high; it was the
first time the film had been shown in Arkansas.—LD

November 2000

My beautiful,

   Damien, that visitation clerk is the sweetest. She said she woke
up in the middle of the night last night thinking of me and so she
thought, "If she comes to my mind, I'll say a little prayer for her."
   I like that very much.

*

Damien, do you remember Ann Wright from Maine? I used to email
her and she sent you books a couple of times—well, she just wrote
and said a reporter from NY is doing a huge feature story about you
for *Rolling Stone*. The writer gave Ann her number for me to call, so I
did—and she's so nice—I told her she needed to talk to Ed Mallett,
but she wants to come here next week to talk to folks. I think it
sounds very good. It's not about celebrities or CDs—it's about proof
of innocence. I am very excited, it sounds so positive. She is very
smart and I have a good feeling about her. We'll see what Ed says.
She is going to call me back tomorrow night.

I love you,

Lorri

November 17, 2000

My love,

They turned the water on for a while last night, so everyone could flush the toilet and get a drink. Today, it's right back off again. I mostly likely won't even have a chance to take a shower before I see you in the morning, so I'm going to stink and won't be able to shave. I hate this place. At least I have a few cups of water saved up.

*

Lorri, you have to constantly envision me being out there. You have to do it, because I can't do it anymore. I can hardly even remember it. And seeing it is a very important part of the process. You have to do it, monkey. It would be best if you could do it for a couple of minutes before you go to sleep every night. You have to do it, Lorri. I can't do it anymore, and it's extremely important.

I am yours,

Damien

December 1, 2000

My beautiful:

I am so happy it's our anniversary. Isn't it wonderful, Damien? I am still amazed it all worked out, and then again I am not—it was what I saw for so long.

*

I wish you could come down with your writings and we could read them together. That would be fun—and we could change things if need be, then I could bring them home and start typing them.

That would be lovely.

Well, it'll still happen one way or another.

Your wife of one year,

Lorri

December 18, 2000

My love,

I'm very proud of you, little monkey. I wish I could have been there for your ceremony. I wish I could have done it with you. You're talking nonsense. I know that Zen master was very impressed with you. All the little things, like forgetting to bow, they're all meaningless. All that matters is your clarity. I'm certain that if you keep practicing with them, one day they will ask you to be a dharma teacher. You'll actually teach people things. It doesn't matter that you didn't get a new koan. Kobutsu said I've passed "Mu," but he still didn't give me another, he told me to bore into it more. He said that even after he passed "Mu," his teacher made him sit with it for 8 more years! That's because it's not something you just "pass" and move on to the next one. You have to attain the heart of the koan, and it has to become part of you. You know what the heart of "Mu" is? It's emptiness. Mu is an emptiness koan. If you dig deep enough into Mu, you will attain emptiness. Then if you keep digging, you will attain emptiness as a form. Mu doesn't just mean "No"—in Japanese Mu means "nothingness" or "emptiness." And there you have it. Joshu said a dog's true nature is emptiness. How does a dog manifest its special kind of dog-emptiness? Woof! Woof! Ja.

I am yours forever,

Damien

January 2, 2001

My beautiful,

I have been on the phone trying to get in touch with people all morning—Scharlette, Ed Mallett, Ed Vedder, Nicole, Steve Bright, John Philipsborn. I will have to take over the management of this case, but I will prevail.

Things are getting accomplished! Finally.

I love you,

Lorri

January 25, 2001

My dearest,

Mara just got back from W. Memphis where she looked at the evidence room. She said she couldn't believe it—they had 30 knives, including 2 kitchen table knives they found in your bedroom. It sickens me that that stuff is still available for everyone to go through. It's not even in plastic bags. Regina Meek watched over her, while she read a *Mysteries of the Bible* book and did crossword puzzles. I really was sickened. As much as I hate to, I'm going to call Ed Mallett tomorrow to see where he is with the appeals.

I love you so much.

I feel frantic—like you should be out NOW.

I love you,

Lorri

February 6, 2001

My lovely one,

   Do you think I really do still "seem evil"? I've tried so hard to get rid of that, and to get it off me the past couple of years. What else can I do? People always watch me, like they're looking for a crack to see into so they can scream, "I saw it! It's still there! I knew it!" Sometimes, it's almost as if damned near everyone is doing that. Just waiting for me to slip. It's an entirely uphill fight.

                                             I am yours forever,

                                                          D.

February 21, 2001

Beloved,

Eddie called last night; he was so excited about the people he has contacted for money. He loves your writings, Damien. I am feeling much calmer today. I think I was a bit frantic yesterday, but I feel much better today.

I am going to put together a "press kit" for you. I am going to try to raise money for your new lawyer. I'll ask anyone I can think of. I feel better just knowing this.

I need to ask you some things. About what to put in it. We'll have to include the *Shambhala Sun* article and some pictures and your writings. I love you so much, Damien. It's one of those days when I am crazy with love for you.

And I will see you soon.

I am happy. I love being married to you. I have learned so much from you.

Don't you worry your beautiful bald head. I am feeling so very calm about everything. When things become clear, then I know what to do.

Forever yours,

Lorri

postscript 2014

Finances. I have never balanced my checkbook, and if asked how I was with accounting, I would probably say it was somewhere at the bottom of my list of talents, along with "plumbing skills." I had no idea. But along with everything else, I learned. I had the help of a friend, Linda Bessette, who gave great advice on setting up accounts and how to raise funds legitimately.

When I went to the bank to set up The Damien Echols Defense Fund, I was told it couldn't be done. After going around and around with various bank employees to no avail, I eventually made an appointment with the bank president. He was intrigued enough by the merits of the case, and my dropping Johnny Depp's name as a generous contributor to the cause (sorry, JD), that he allowed the account to be opened.

I was very, very strict about funds. They were not to be used for anything but casework. I remember gossip on the Internet accusing me of all kinds of fiscal mischief—that was before I stopped reading message boards. I kept accounts and copies of all checks and even wrote thank-you letters to everyone who donated. Eventually I became too exhausted to write to everyone, but it felt good while it lasted.

We ran a letter on WM3.org that resulted in funding coming in from all over the world, but there was never a surplus, and I was forever asking. It wasn't pleasant. But that didn't stop me; I was on a mission, and pride wasn't an option.

An especially stressful money moment came when Dennis Riordan came on board as Damien's lead attorney. We needed $200k in three weeks. I'll never forget it, I took to sleeping with tennis balls under my neck, because someone told me it would demolish the knots forming there. We raised it; after Ed Vedder called his entire phone book, Johnny and Henry [Rollins] ponied up—and when we were $50K out, I took out personal loans for the rest.

—Lorri

February 2001

Dearest beautiful one,

You'd better straighten up, Mister Moody. I got 2 letters, well, the last two letters have been sad and scantly a page long. I am going to rough you up on Friday. Enough of this—you must come back—there is too much joy to be had, Damien—joy in love. And you are so loved.

I'll fix you on Friday. I'll give you head shivers and a shoulder massage, I'll clean your ears and anything on your face, I'll inspect your head and all parts of your body.

You will be loved past the point of your endurance.

I know I have some work to do with you. I can tell. You little thing.

I love you, beautiful,

L.

April 4, 2001

My lovely one,

   Three thousand dollars is pretty good, considering that the fund
has been open for about a week. Then if we get that $25,000, that
would be $28,000. Very good. Lorri, no one else could do this except
you. No one. They're not capable. Even if I don't always say it, I'm
very, very thankful for what you are doing. You will be the one to
save me. I don't want you to think that what you're doing isn't being
recognized because it is.

I am yours forever,

D.

April 10, 2001

My lovely ladybug,

   This morning when I woke up I was soooo happy, because the birds had started building a nest in my window. They must have been busy throughout the night, making trips to bring the grass. I couldn't stop thinking about how I would get to sit and look at the baby birds when they hatch, see them grow, and watch the big birds sit on the eggs. I thought that even if for some reason they decided not to finish it, it was still nice to be able to look at the grass they left behind. Then, as I was doing my morning sitting, they came back and took all the grass away! They didn't leave even a tiny scrap behind. They took everything their little beaks could get a hold of. I couldn't believe it. Much disappointment. Why did they have to do that?

I am yours forever,

Damien

April 26, 2001

My dearest Damien,

Your case was reversed and remanded by the Supreme Court today. Ed Mallett says it is the best we could've hoped for. He told me to tell you that. I will explain more tonight, it was just sent back to Judge Burnett for more work on his part.

I want to talk to Rob Owen, so I can understand more what is up.

Joe Berlinger sent $2,500—sound familiar? It's the $2,500.00 owed to you anyway!!! Can you believe it?! People are too funny.*

Lorri

---

* Damien was offered $2,500 for his appearance in *Paradise Lost 2*, which for various reasons he couldn't accept at the time of filming, so it was funny that Joe's donation was so very similar . . .—LD

May 7, 2001

Dearest beautiful,

   I just love you so much, Damien, and I get scared that I'm not going to keep up with everything or do the right thing or not say the right thing or be the right person.

Your wife,

Lorri

May 14, 2001

My dearest Damien,

    I just sent $5,200 more dollars to the trust account!! That really is $17,000—now—if some of that BIG money would come in!!

    It's so nice of people to send money. Some are sending weekly or monthly $5, $10, or $50. I'm writing to all of them. It really is the best.

    I want to go home and do yoga. But there is more time to be spent here. Time to stop wishing and be here.

Forever yours,

L.

May 30, 2001

Dearest one,

We get an oral argument for the writ of error—Mallett is going to have Rob Owen do it, which I think is smart—Ed wouldn't know what he was doing.

This just in . . . the Innocence Project (Barry Scheck) is now working with the civil case in NY to try to get DNA stuff. How interesting.

I love you, beautiful,

Lorri

June 8, 2001

Lovely Monkey,

I can't believe it's already Thursday. I see you tomorrow, and another week is gone. It's amazing how time passes so quickly. It doesn't seem there's any way that I could have been here for all these years. Perhaps, soon I will be with you.

*

Perhaps they'll rule on Rule 37 soon. I'm not expecting anything from it, but it'll be nice to be out of state court. Out of the hands of morons.

I am yours forever,

Damien

June 14, 2001

Dearest beautiful one,

Some guy named T. J. Wilford has started posting on the website—Jene called and told me. He was friends with Ryan Clark before the murders, and has been telling all the horrible things he saw JMB do to Christopher. According to him, that kid was horribly abused, and so hyper he was hard to be around. I am trying to put him in touch with the investigator from Parker's firm.

Maybe something will happen.

I love you, beautiful,

Lorri

September 25, 2001

Dearest,

I read John Philipsborn's document last night. I really have a much better feel for what happened in that courtroom. It made me very, very sad that you had no one to help you.

I couldn't sleep very well. I wish everyone could read that thing— it was very good. I still have some more to read.

I talked to the new investigator today. I'm going to meet with him next week—I'm going to tell him everything in Mara's book.

I love you, beautiful,

L.

October 9, 2001

My Love,

I know it's hard on you, these times. Still, you have to listen to me, Lorri. I know what I'm doing. I had thought this chance gone forever. I had given up on it, thought it gone never to be seen again. Imagine my surprise to see that the doors were slammed wide open this year, a full invitation. And I know that this is the last time it will ever be so. If I lose it now, I lose it period. Yeah, it's hard for you now, but just imagine if I can come to you a hundred thousand times better than ever before. Imagine feeling things for me a hundred times stronger than you do now, and being with me forever. Do you not consider that worth a little pain?

I'm more ready right now than I've ever been. Zen, the Tao, Vajrayana, the Golden Dawn, the old ways, and Gnosticism, Sufism, and Catholicism. So many bases from which to draw power. I'll walk right in like I own the place.

You just be good, Lorri. I love you more than words can say and nothing can ever change that. You just need to calm down and stop worrying so much. I know more of you than you know.

I love you,

Damien

October 31, 2001

My love,

Curious to know what this mysterious calling benefactor said last night. I don't trust him. "Oh, I just happen to have an extra million that I found in the pocket of one of my old tuxedos—you can have it."

*

I love you, Lorri. No matter what you think, I do just want things to go back to normal. For you to be OK.

I love you,

D.

November 13, 2001

Dearest Damien,

First of all—I am not depressed—and secondly, I have no desire
to go out and "do more" in this place. The thought of going to a
café or sitting somewhere "drinking coffee" or something like that
sickens me. Yes, I know I used to do that in NY—but I was searching
for something and I am not searching anymore. Damien, I was sad
because of the things I have been talking to you about over the last
few weeks—I'm not "depressed." I know Susan means well, but she
can't understand. She doesn't know what it means to "have" what
you have always wanted—to know that it is everything to you
and you can just be enveloped by it. Even if things are sad. It's still
just you that I want. I found it to be funny—both you and her telling
me I need to "get out more." I don't.

If something occurs to me that I want to do, then I shall do it. I
have what I want. That is my life with you.

You need to just stop with your meddling. I mean it.

Some people just don't know—but you do.

I love you,

L.

December 14, 2001

My lovely one,

You're entirely too much lately. I can hardly even take it. Just the very sight of you hurts my heart, with all your stuff. You're a real person. I'm not. Just seeing all your business reminds me that I'm not a real person. The closest I can come is this cartoon character. It just makes me love you a thousand times more. I'll be very glad when tomorrow arrives and I get to see your beautiful face.

What's the next unpleasant thing we have to deal with? There's always something lurking just around the corner. That's how I keep track of time these days, by how long it is until the next unpleasant thing. Someone coming, or something I have to do, or some other pure bullshit. It's about time to be getting the hell up out of here. There are things we have to do, and they're not getting done here.

I love you,

D.

December 18, 2001

My Lovely One,

    This weekend I had terrible fun with you. It's torture not to begin immediately calling again first thing this morning. You're all the baby animals wrapped up in one. "Will you be my friend?" You nearly killed me when you said that. My heart blew up. Of course I will be your friend, little critter. Forever and ever.

I love you,

Damien

December 21, 2001

My beloved Damien,

    I mean it about the mail thing—if you write me one letter a week—or even if you don't do that—I will be happy. I would much rather get a letter from you that you were excited to write than letters that are drudgery for you. And I am so completely honest about that. With no hidden tricks—it's exactly as it should be.

I love you,

Lorri

January 3, 2002

Dearest Damien,

That's another thing about last night. I was looking around and I thought—if Damien were sitting here beside me, I would be so proud to be with him—he is so beautiful, your lovely face and body—but just the feel of you.

You really are mine, I have claimed you, but I know I must give you up to all and everything. It has been the work of my life. I used to think it was getting you out of there—that is a job—my work is to let go, but still have you. I know it will be the best life and you will love me even more than you could even imagine.

There are no more excuses.

I love you,

Lorri

January 15, 2002

My lovely one,

Most nervous about meeting your mom and dad. I guess they won't get my letter until after they've already been here. Isn't it hard to believe they're actually coming here? Just to think, I'm meeting your parents!

I love you,

D.

January 23, 2002

My dearest Damien,

My heart hurts terribly. I love you so much. Seeing you with my parents yesterday gave me a whole new appreciation for you and for them. My parents are surprising me lately.

This morning my dad said, "Seems like you married yourself a pretty good boy." I laughed and said I already knew that. He said, "I only wish he didn't listen to that 'heavy metal'—I don't know much about it, but it seems to get blamed for a lot of things—like Columbine."

I told him just like everything else, he shouldn't judge it til he hears it.

They really like you. I think they are breathing a big sigh of relief—now they know you, I'm so glad!! I kept looking at you thinking of how proud I am to be married to you.

I'm a little emotional this morning.

I noticed yesterday, how you were very much yourself—yet you made allowances for my mom and dad. You were such the gentleman. I am forever amazed by you, Damien, and I can't stop this overwhelming love I have for you.

I have to work really hard to get you out of there!!!

Your wife,

Lorri

January 24, 2002

My love,

   You know what? I think I miss your parents. I really like them, as
long as it's in small doses. I wouldn't mind at all if they were to
come back for a return visit.

                                             I love you,

                                             Damien

June 6, 2002

My dearest,

I got three letters from you yesterday. I couldn't get to sleep last night, so I reread them very late at night. I love your letters, Damien. There is always at least one thing in all of them that rivets me. It's been a long time since I slept with your letters under my pillow, but I did last night. I can't get close enough.

*

I believe "Miss Manners" is a Zen master. You'd know if you read it.

Your wife,

L.

June 28, 2002

My lovely one,

I hopped out of bed and tried to call you first thing this
morning—no answer! Y'all are out and about early on this day. I
miss you too much, Lorri. I just want to hear your voice. All day
long I lie here in bed, thinking about how I always self-destruct.
Sometimes, lately I think you're like a test. Here I've been given this
wife who is perfect in every way, in ways I didn't even realize at
first—like not knowing that every other woman on the planet
apparently has cellulite—and it's a test just to see exactly how long it
takes before I fuck myself off. Sooner or later, it's bound to happen.
Even knowing what a rare, magickal, wonderful thing I possess
—I'm still a time bomb, waiting to fuck myself. I just want to make
you happy. Lately, when you say things about how you want to
spend your life making me happy, I feel a wave of sadness roll over
me, feeling like I'm not worth shit, I'm fucked up, worthless. I want
so desperately to say the same things to you, but it feels as if they
would be so false coming from me.

Forever,

D.

July 5, 2002

My lovely one,

   You truly are a remarkable thing. I keep thinking of you offering
to let Domini stay with you and try to find a place here. That is
something that no one else would do. I'm so lucky to have you.
There's nothing like you anywhere else. You keep asking why I'm
married to you and not someone else. It's because of what you are,
Lorri. You and all your magick and monkey business. You are the
greatest thing. Just thinking of you right now, and all you do, it
makes my heart hurt. I love you, Lorri. I never forget what you are.

*

Holidays are so weird in here. Especially the feeding times, only two
meals. I really don't think breakfast foods are very good for you,
except for oatmeal. The rest of it just smells like it does more
damage than good—eggs, biscuits, all that. Today is Jason's birthday.
He was a 4th of July baby.

I am yours forever,

Damien

July 9, 2002

Dearest Damien,

Cally sent a note this morning. All it said was . . . "How does a guy in prison spend so much money?" You know she should be smacked, or her head nuzzled for that. I'm sure you will get a like question.

I love you, beautiful.

L.

September 12, 2002

Dearest one,

Your case is now officially on hold. That was the big news today.
J. Burnett has 60 days to do something about the DNA. We shall see.
I'm so glad, it's exactly what we need to happen.

I actually called your mother and told her the hearing was
cancelled. I must be very lucid today—I feel like doing things.

*

I've missed you horribly today. I know I say that in every letter—but
I do. I miss you so much in every letter.

Your wife,

Lorri

September 18, 2002

My dearest,

I forgot to tell you, I got that book *Dear Scott, Dearest Zelda*—the love letters of F. Scott Fitzgerald and his wife, Zelda Fitzgerald. I have always liked her—it'll be fun to read, but sad. She spent much of their life together in a sanatorium. She was schizophrenic. But she was so lovely and very smart and creative. It'll be a good read.

I would hate it if anyone ever published our letters!! Ha ha, can you imagine?! There would be 5,000 of them! Probably 7,000 in all!

Your wife,

Lorri

October 1, 2002

My Lovely Monkey,

This prison life is killing me. As soon as I wake up, I need a nap, and there are 100 and 1 little aches and pains scattered throughout my body that are just bad enough to annoy and make me uncomfortable. Like my knees. I'm getting old very quickly. All the concrete, steel, and stupidity is just sucking the life right out of me. All my chi and youth. I need ankle-deep shag carpeting and paneled walls, window-unit air conditioners, dark rooms and blue lightbulbs, soft black clothes and hair on my head. Then slowly, the process would stop.

Monkey bread. That's what you took to your little party. A fresh baked loaf of monkey bread. Last night I kept smiling to myself, thinking of you on Friday wanting me to just sit and hold your little foot up, just suspended in the air while you played. And your little instructions of "Don't do anything, just hold it there and let me be safe." Every time I think of it, it nearly kills me.

They're training a new mail woman this morning. If I'm not mistaken, I think they said it's the real mail woman, from the post office in Tucker. I guess we'll just have to see how it's going to work out. I still wish they'd just keep the one who's been doing it.

I just had a lunch of fried chicken and blueberry cake. I'm so exhausted, I believe I'm going to have to take a nap. And I haven't even done anything today. I must finish this book. And write to the abbess, and Terry and Theresa. Among others. It's a hard day not doing work calls. I miss you terribly.

I am yours forever.

D.

p.s. The phone is broken. Just in case they don't get it fixed tonight, I wanted to make sure you know.

October 2, 2002

Dearest,

I went to the [Arkansas Coalition to Abolish the Death Penalty] meeting today. I'm supposed to meet with Frank King* about the meeting with Norris over some of these things. They may have to file another lawsuit. I'm more than ready to work on it. They were pretty nice at the meeting, and Freddie Nixon told me she has been hearing horrible things as well. Maybe we can actually accomplish something.

Your wife,

Lorri

---

* Frank King was the deacon from the nearby Catholic church who used to visit the prison. Freddie Nixon was on the board of the Arkansas Coalition to Abolish the Death Penalty, but also a friend and support to the guys on death row.—LD

October 3, 2002

My loveliest monkey,

There's a tree frog taking a sunbath on my window. He looks like it's about time to hibernate. For some reason it reminds me of last night—there was one single star in the sky that was bright enough for me to see it through my window. A very rare thing. With all the spotlights and filth caked up on the window. When I saw it, I was amazed.

*

I must do a work call today. "Operator, please put me through to the monkey house."

I love you,

D.

October 5, 2002

Dearest,

I get so anxious sometimes—I feel like getting you out of there is just around the corner (like Halloween) but I want it now. You would think after (almost) 8 years, I would have learned patience.

Things are changing down there. I could really feel it yesterday. I hope they get so much better for you guys.

Your wife,

L.

December 5, 2002

My lovely anniversary monkey,

Lorri, I don't want you to volunteer to help with those Christmas sacks. I don't want you to see back here. I don't want everyone leering at you, and I don't want you to see these cages. Not so much for yourself, because I know you can handle it. But for me. It's bad enough with you having to see me in this environment when we're together—but back here, the way it is—that's 100 times worse.

*

3 years married, little thing. That doesn't really mean anything because we should be celebrating 6 years. We should have just gotten married as soon as we met. I can feel the thread.

Happy anniversary, my beautiful wife,

Damien

January 13, 2003

Dearest Damien,

No word yet from the *Dr. Phil* folks; it's still early out there, though.* Gwynne was going to watch the documentaries over the weekend. I wrote a draft of the letter to Johnny Depp, and heard from Joe about coming to Arkansas. He says he thinks it's a very good idea. I only wish we could all meet together. You should meet with them first.

I feel much better today, not so frustrated as I did over the weekend. Things feel almost back to normal, more manageable.

*

Something has to happen, we have to figure it out. You have to help me.

I love you so much. I can just feel there is another way of doing this . . .

I love you,

L.

---

* Dr. Phil was trying to get us to do a show, or a series of shows, about the case. Thank heavens we decided against it. It wouldn't be until 2007 that we started doing media in earnest with some guidance.—LD

January 15, 2003

My love,

   You must calm down, Lorri. Working yourself up into such a
frenzy isn't going to help either of us. Everything will soon be as it
should be. I've allowed things to get too far out of my control—
once upon a time, those *Dr. Phil* people would have come and asked
me. Now everyone goes to the lawyers or to the website or to Mara
Leveritt. No one even bothers to ask me anymore. That has to be
fixed.

Yours forever,

D.

February 4, 2003

Dearest,

    A girl from Seattle came here today to help with the bike master plan. We started talking and she knew all about the WM3 through Eddie Vedder. She was amazed that you weren't out of prison yet. See, if we don't keep things out there, people just think they have been taken care of.

I love you, beautiful,

L.

March 5, 2003

My lovely one,

Every week at practice you have to do the Kwan Seum Bosals for me to get out of here so we can be together. I'll try to remind you every week.

They started passing out razors that won't cut anything again. They're trying to save money. They won't cut, but then they take it out on us for not shaving. If they don't go back to the others, I'll have to go see the doctor about getting a doctor's order for not shaving.

Those lawyers make me nervous. I just don't trust them at all. Now that they've stopped answering at all, there's no telling what they might do. I really hope those other lawyers want to come on the case. Someone who actually wants to work.

I love you,

D.

March 19, 2003

Dearest,

I hate it that you are so stressed. I really have to watch it, because my heart can hurt so much sometimes, just thinking of what you have to endure in there. I find myself getting so angry at how much time everything takes, and then it does no good. I'm trying to deal with it all better.

I just wish things were better in there.

At least they got "Healthy Choice" ice cream!

Nicole said in a note that her first order of business is getting us to sleep better at night—and the second order is getting us to sleep together at night!! I liked that very much.

I miss you so much.

Your wife,

L.

March 25, 2003

My lovely one,

I'm so exhausted. It's seeped into my bones, and saturated every muscle in my body. It's an almost constant feeling these days, making me miserable. I just can't get enough rest, and it messes up everything else. Lorri, when I'm sleeping, you better not mess with me. Pestering and waking me up. I mean it, I need my rest. I feel like an old man. As if I should be bundled up, sitting next to a fireplace, dozing. It scares me, wondering how it'll be at the age of 50, 60, or 70, if it's already like this now.

I love you,

D.

April 1, 2003

My lovely one,

Lorri, I loved, dearly loved listening to you get ready for bed last night. That is something I will never, ever forget.

I love you,

D.

May 7, 2003

My loveliest,

The letters to Domini and Seth went out this morning. It's hard for me to write to Seth, because I never know what he'll understand and what he won't. I told him that we both have to be good because our actions reflect on each other. That we must behave with honor, so that others who know us can't say anything bad about us, and we can each have pride—he in his father, me in my son. I know it's hard to think of such things when you're young and things aren't going like you want, but that's when being strong comes in. I really do think he should be enrolled in something like a children's martial arts class. Something to teach him the discipline that those around him lack.

I love you, little lotus,

D.

May 15, 2003

My lovely thing,

Last night I dreamed I was out somewhere and was attacked by that guy that always runs at me in court. He grabbed me from behind, and I was furious, because I kept thinking, "When is this shit ever going to end?" He tried to spray some kind of acid in my ear and I started doing everything I could to cripple him for life—smash his knees, break his arms—I can't remember the end of it.

*

I hate all of these people here so much. Inmates and guards both. I'm so sick of having to deal with them, of even having to speak to them. In 6 months, the DNA testing will be at least partially completed. Even if it doesn't get us out, it'll still be another hole in their bullshit to build on.

Lorri, you have no idea how proud of you I am. When you talk to people like that newswoman and they see how smart you are, how beautiful you are. I know everyone is always amazed to see me with such a woman. I definitely married up and everyone knows it.

I love you forever,

D.

May 22, 2003

Dearest,

I got a letter from you yesterday saying you "married up." Hah!!
We are both the same, if anything I married up!! My dad is so proud
of you. He asks about you every time he calls. He asked how old
you were going to be at your next birthday. I said, "29"—he said,
"He's probably the most mature 29-year-old you'll ever know!" I
laughed and said he didn't know—you were a baby. He didn't laugh!
Ha ha ha!!

I sat down last night and got all my financial stuff straightened
out. It felt good to do it. I still have some work on the defense fund,
but I'll figure it out.

                                        I love you horribly,

                                                    L.

AFFIDAVIT

STATE OF ARKANSAS)
)
COUNTY OF JEFFERSON)

I, Damien Echols _____, after being first duly sworn, do hereby swear, depose and state: I am being beaten, abused, threatened, and tormented by members of staff at the A.D.C. I've been told that if I tell anyone, I will be beaten even worse, or killed. They are even attempting to prevent me from contacting the outside world so that I cannot tell anyone. I've asked for help from staff members and the leutenant and have been ignored or told to "shut up".

CC. Lyndall Stout, channel 4 news   Asst. Warden James, A.D.C.
    Mara Leveritt, Arkansas Times   Warden Evans, A.D.C.
    Betsey Write, A.C.L.U.   Lorri Davis.

I further state that all statements contained herein are true to the best of my knowledge, information and belief.

NAME: Damien Echols _____

DATE: _____

SIGNATURE: Damien Echols

SUBSCRIBED and sworn to before me this _____ day of _____, 200____.

_____
NOTARY PUBLIC

My Commission expires: _____

My Lovely one,

You have to be okay and be strong, beautious thing.
This will work out, too. We'll deal with these people and put an end
to everything they're doing. I'm sending you this affidavit — if they do anything
at all, like write me up, you immediately send a copy to Betsey Write
and Lyndall Stout. Don't waste a single second. If James wants to
lie and cover things up, we'll bring them to light. You can't hesitate.
He's just been sitting there waiting for the chance to hurt me. So we're
going to let everyone know how corrupt they are.

You were so beautiful today, with your shirt with the
back cut out. I knew it was just for me when I saw it. I wanted
to bite your little skin. You needed it, sweetest of the monkeys.

As soon as you get this, you should immediately go to the
director and ask him why I'm being investigated, why they want to
write me a disciplinary for how the phone company runs their business.
I don't make the phone company route their calls through England, so why
am I being punished, when I'm not even the only one who's numbers
work like that. Cut this shit off before it even gets started.
We weren't forwarding the calls — that's the way the phone company
works. I just called Kelly Canary and am getting her on the job,
too. This will all work out.

I'm holding you close, little monkey skins. You are
right in my heart, held tight. You have no fear of that. I'll be
writing to you every day until we're talking again. I love you so
very much, beautiful thing.

I am yours forever,
D.

October 14, 2003

Dearest,

   Too close—you and your visitor are getting too close. He has no idea what "close" is. And the ridiculousness of such a statement, "You and your wife are getting too close." It's so ridiculous I can hardly bear to give it any more thought, other than to laugh at it.

I love you, beauteous,

L.

November 18, 2003

Dear Monkus Minimus,

Lorri, these lawyers are scaring me. I can feel it in my bones that
they're messing up. They have one year to get my appeal before the
federal court, yet they're going to be spending the next 6 months
resubmitting it to the Arkansas court system. It doesn't sound right
to me. I can't even call to find out what's going on. I need a new
lawyer. I've been asking everyone here and they all say that after the
Rule 37 was denied they went into federal court. I don't think they
know what they're doing.

Lorri, even during the stress I love you so much my heart hurts.

I am yours forever,

Damien

December 4, 2003

My lovely wife,

It's our anniversary! It doesn't seem like there's any way that it could be 4 years now. There would have to be lots of treats today. I would get you one of those giant chocolate chip cookies and would have "happy anniversary" on it. You would also have a bundle of helium balloons with pictures of cavorting creatures on them, and attached to colorful ribbons. There would be all sorts of lingerie and shoes of the high-heeled variety for presents and maybe a few items from the sub-shop.* There will be no tailless cats spilling protein drinks, but there will be lots of business. I'm terribly messed up today. I've been constantly looking at a picture of you today, where you're wearing tight jeans and have all your makeup on. I fear you would have to have an anniversary ass smacking.

*

That lawyer has to come on the case. Time is ticking away. We need him now. At least they now have a new chief justice in the Arkansas Supreme Court. I'm not holding my breath for anything, but at least there's a small chance of something going differently. We need a lawyer.

I love you,

D.

---

* I'm talking about Submission, a bondage shop online at the time, not sandwiches.—DE

December 10, 2003

My Dearest Damien:

   This is our 7th birthday together. I can remember when we had our first, and I said it would be the first of the rest of them. I was as sure of that then as I am of it today.

   I love you in ways I can't even fathom sometimes. We've been through so much, and it only makes us stronger and want more and more and more. I hope you have a great day—just know you are loved more than humanly possible, and you will be forever—

Your wife,

Lorri

January 21, 2004

My lovely creature,

Lorri, those little grey hairs I found on your head last Thursday have caused me a great deal of anxiety. I keep thinking they're the result of all the stress you have to deal with because of these lawyers. I'm scared it's going to wear you down or make you sick. I'm just so glad you're doing yoga and eating better. I hope you're not feeling like I do when I say years are being taken off my life. I need to be able to take care of you. To give you a rubdown and green tea. Soon, I will. I felt a wave of it roll over me just now. That I'll be out soon.

How have you turned me into a happy, laughing thing? There was a time when I never smiled and had no idea what being happy meant, but I can barely remember it. Now, I only know constant giggling and antics. There is nothing but playing now. And you are an infectious monkey. You are spreading monkeydom everywhere you go. People change to monkeys right before my eyes.

I am yours forever,

D.

February 3, 2004

My Beautiful, sleepy, short-tailed monkey,

You're in the meeting with Dennis Riordan right now. I'm
desperately hoping he signs on. I'm sending you all the good luck.
Lorri, you are the only person on earth who could do something
like this. No one else has the will, strength, or competence. You're
insane talking about who you "can't compete with." That is literally
insane.

I am going to start trying to send you more letters. In my mind I
see the *Pirates of the Caribbean* monkey contentedly clutching a letter,
much like Tellis with her letter. This is why I haven't had the chance
to write one single page more on my book—because I can't get
caught up on letters.

One of the polls says that if the elections were held today, Kerry
and Bush would be almost even—Kerry has 46%, Bush has 44%.
And Kerry is against the death penalty. I've decided to add my
endorsement to whoever wins the Democratic primary—with every
letter I write, I will tell people to vote Democrat. Since I can't vote
myself, I shall attempt to influence the vote of others. You should do
so in your thank-you notes.

I finally finished the Nijinsky book this morning. In a way, he
makes me angry because he was one of those people like my sister
that can't do anything for themselves. He had a pretty horrible life.

I'm desperately looking for something I can send you for
Valentine's Day. It's almost upon us again. It's absolutely one of the

most stressful times of year for me. Every year it grows harder than the one before. I don't even have a piece of red paper to cut out little hearts. I have to find something for such a beauteous creature.

I love you.

D.

February 17, 2004

Dearest,

I don't know why I get insecure. I don't doubt you for a second in your love for me. I think my whole life I've always thought men were never satisfied with even the love of their lives. I never believed that a man was capable of true and complete love. I always believed they were always looking for something else, better sex, a more beautiful body, whatever . . .

All this to say, it's me. You have never done anything to make me feel this way. Actually, the opposite. I still feel that way about every other man, though.

I know women are probably guilty of equal behavior; I just focus on men.

I want to fix it, because it doesn't matter and it just makes me sad and needy. You always handle it so well. You now know what to do with me. I don't know why I've been thinking about that lately.

Your wife,

Lorri

March 6, 2004

My loveliest of the monkey-like creatures,

    Tomorrow I see you. The time goes by so quickly here. It seems that I do nothing except get ready to call you or get ready to see you. That's how I like it. It makes me feel more connected.

I love you,

D.

March 16, 2004

My lovely creature,

Enclosed with this letter you should find a page from the new Brooks Brothers ad. Is it not amazing? When I opened the magazine and saw it, it really was like something went through me. I can't stop looking at it. It really was almost like a religious experience. I hate to even fold the page. Once I'm out of here, I don't want any clothes in my closet that aren't Brooks Brothers. When I was a kid I had a ton of Brooks Brothers stuff. A preacher who lived near us had a grandson who was a little older than me, and when he outgrew his clothes, they gave them all to me. They would come to visit us two or three times a year, and they would have a big garbage bag of clothes every time. Now I want it to be my own personal brand. This suit in this ad is a work of art. See how subtle it is? But very powerful. I must have it. Next I will send you the picture of some Brooks Brothers slacks I must have. This suit is the epitome of style—you could have worn it in the 1920s, the 1980s, or now in 2004.

I love you,

D.

March 24, 2004

Dearest Beauteous:

About my sisters not "approving" of you. As if that meant anything—actually, yours very much loves you—in the way you can love someone she doesn't know. She doesn't write or send things because she doesn't even do that for me!! She told me she thinks about writing you all the time, and she prays for you every day.

Seth will do fine with my parents. Don't you worry. He was actually really good when he was with me—it's wayward energy (like Jennifer and his mother) that he reacts to—Seth will be OK. He was good with you—

Damien, you always leave an amazing impression on people—you truly are a gentleman, and a Southern one at that. I love that my dad loves and respects you. He told me the other day that you've endured things he would've caved over. I wish you could really know how proud I am of you. You amaze me daily. You automatically know the right things—your fashion sense, music—it was in you, already.

I love you, beauteous.

Your wife,

Lorri

April 6, 2004

My loveliest,

In a way I am jealous of you getting to read this book* a few pages at a time, because for you it will be like back in the beginning. Back then every single word was amazing because we didn't know anything of each other, it was all fresh and new. Now, you'll be learning little bits and scraps all the time that will make things more clear for you. I love sending them to you, and I wish I could see the look on your face as you read every word. I have written until my fingers are stiff and painful, and my wrist feels crooked. For the past few days I've written from the moment the light came on in the morning until the moment the light goes off at night.

Your adoring husband,

D.

---

* This was the draft of my first self-published book, *Almost Home.*—DE

April 13, 2004

My dearest beauteous,

I've been getting your book and reading about you really stays
with me. It goes into my bones, and sometimes I get so mad I can
hardly stand it . . . Sometimes, I'm amazed how wonderful you are
considering what you were born to—but you knew what you were
doing from the beginning, you knew what you had to learn.

It makes me feel very fortunate. For all the blocks my parents
have, at least I was safe and didn't feel in a scary place. No wonder
you've always sought relationships that are "no bones."

I'm looking forward to reading more.

Maybe someday, I'll write things about me for you (I would never
publish it, not interesting to other people).

I'm first going to have to start drawing again. It makes me happy,
and you deserve things.

I love you,

Lorri

April 21, 2004

My loveliest,

My writing is slowing down now. Or mayhap my mind just isn't so sharp today because I was up all night wrestling with those rats. I hate those bastards. Writing this book is doing something to me. It's bringing me closer to the outside world, making me remember what it was like to be free, and making me want it more. Lorri, I had really forgotten. Isn't that strange? I didn't think it was true, but I had. Something in my heart is an animal, and it has been kicked awake like an old dog. It's awake now, and it's smacking its jaws. It's time to get up to business, and everyone knows you can't spell business without SIN. I remember life. The music is helping me, too. Ever since we've been here, I haven't felt the urge to listen to the radio. Now, I can't turn it off. I listen to it all night. I'm waking up, you little monkey. How did I ever get lulled into such a deep sleep? Now, it's time to clap your clappers and snap your snappers.

*

My mail seems to be slowing down. Not so much of it is coming anymore. Anna's movie needs to hurry up and come out so people can be reminded.*

I love you,

D.

---

* Anna Phelan, screenwriter for *Gorillas in the Mist* and many other movies, wrote an early script for *Devil's Knot* by Mara Leveritt. It was, to my mind, a great and truthful depiction of the case and our situation, although sadly it was ultimately shelved.—DE

April 29, 2004

My beauteous beauteous,

Mom and Dad were so happy to see you. Mom got all dressed up, Damien—she rolled her hair the night before and bought new clothes. It broke my heart. I almost cried when they weren't going to let her in. You could tell she was really upset.

I love you, Damien.

Lorri

June 17, 2004

My lovely,

   You are supposed to give this little diagram to Theresa. It's the place I was sleeping the night of May 5th.

                                        I love you,

                                                 D.

June 28, 2004

Dearest beauteous,

   You'll be getting a letter from a woman in North Carolina who is doing a benefit. She is really doing a lot. I just wanted to give you a heads-up, 'cause she'll probably make a lot of money for the fund. We may have Dad and Lucy paid off before we know it!! That will make me so happy.

   Theresa and Dennis want me to come to SF after the weekend in Seattle. That will be a long time gone. We'll have to talk about it.

I love you!

L.

August 2, 2004

My dearest,

Neil was trying to talk to me about his exploits with spanking and I shut it down. I will not be discussing such things with him. Only you. I couldn't believe. Some girl from Texas he spanked all over San Francisco.

He also asked if I'd ever had phone sex. I let a second go by, then said, "I have a husband in prison!"

Your wife,

Lorri

August 5, 2004

Damien,

    I just sent a letter about the phones to Betsey. I've spent over $57,000 on the phones since we met!! Isn't that amazing?

Your wife,

Lorri

September 14, 2004

Loveliest of the baby animals,

    Lorri, are you ever amazed by the fact that I'm innocent and on death row? Sometimes when I think about it, it "blows my mind." How could this happen? Things like this aren't supposed to happen.

Your adoring husband,

D.

September 16, 2004

Dearest,

   Damien, all I want is to have you home. It has actually been causing me physical pain because I miss you so much. I just want this over. I just want you here.

I love you horribly,

L.

October 19, 2004

My loveliest,

I did go outside today after all. I was so exhausted from walking
around in circles for an hour that it made me sick. I'm not used to
anything but this cell. That's how it will be for a great while when I
first get out, too. I'll need a cane. I came back in and fell into a deep
sleep.

*

Now, they're not even drying our clothes. They pull them straight
out of the washer and send them to us soaking wet. We've had
pancakes for the last three meals, because they've run out of
supplies in the kitchen. They've got enough pancake mix to last
forever, it seems. That's why I say I'll never eat another pancake
once I'm out of here.

Do you remember that guard who had me sign the copy of
Mara's book for him? He killed himself. A single gunshot. I can still
feel him around. It plagues me. It's one of those things I'll see
forever.

I love you,

D.

December 2, 2004

Dearest baby Monkus,

    'Tis the first day of December, one of the two greatest months of the year. The other is January. In an ideal world we would alternate between December and January, and the rest of the months would cease to exist. They're nestled right in the gray heart of winter, buffered on one side by November, and on the other by February. The summer can't sneak up on you. The magick of December and January is like living inside a snow globe.

*

When I was a kid, people were amazed by how fast I was. In Mississippi, people used to stand on the porch and watch me running around. They'd say things like, "Look at his legs!" An old black woman used to call me a rabbit. I want to run again. Not hopping up and down on a concrete floor, or jogging around New York, like Susan, but real running. Through the woods. Through real earth, where you feel your feet dig in for traction. Where your body feels like a machine, everything flowing smoothly. It's hard to even imagine such a thing now.

    I have a cavity in my wisdom tooth. That settles it. Now, it has to come out. Drat! I am terrified.

I LOVE you,

Damien

January 19, 2005

My lovely,

It's time to start doing something, Lorri. You can start with that building class. It's time to start growing. You are withering up. All those things in you that are so magickal and that make my heart explode are drying up. Everything is going out and nothing is coming in. It's scaring me, Lorri. Very much so. Every day it becomes harder and harder to write these letters because there's not even anything to write about. I can't bring new life in, Lorri. It's impossible for me, I'm helpless. It's up to you. You've got your drawing supplies, and you can sign up for that building class. Then you can sign up for one of those martial arts classes you've talked about off and on. This is one more thing closing in, suffocating, making life harder. This is one thing that you can actually do something about. And I already know that we will fight over this. It's going to cause a great deal of stress, because you've become so used to doing nothing that you want to continue to do it. And, if you do, you will kill us both. You've dug yourself into a rut, and it's hard to get you to move. I'm scared and I'm angry and I'm stressed out. I can't give one more fucking inch or I'm going to snap. My fucking spine is breaking, so please don't make this any harder than it already is. You have to move, Lorri. Please.

You need art classes, too. Drawing, painting, art history, art appreciation. You're not doing either of us any favors by allowing every trace of ambition to die.

This is the trap that all married people fall into. They stop changing, stop growing, stop learning, and stop doing anything.

I have to write some letters and get the economy flowing again. My head is pounding and I'm tired.

I love you,

D.

January 20, 2005

Dearest baby contraption,

I love the idea of something happening in NY with Dennis. It
could be a really good fund-raiser.

I just learned we lost in state court.

It's time to fight. I've had it.

Your wife,

Lorri

February 26, 2005

My dearest:

I want so much to tell you how much I love you. Sometimes, I watch movies or read stories and they make me realize how lucky and how magickal my life is because I have you. You know me so well, and my love for you can never be shaken. I think of every aspect of you and my heart goes weak. That feeling of falling.

You said this morning that there are no longer any 15-page letters—Damien, don't you realize that there is a constant? Every hour, every minute is spent thinking of you, or doing something that has to do with you, or longing for you, or talking to you, or writing to you.

My life is you, and my heart will forever belong to you. You've taught me so much about love. You are gallant and brave and I marvel at how you continue to intrigue and inspire me. How did I ever deserve you?!

I will forever and ever find you and love you. You are mine.

I love you more than I could ever say.

Your wife,

Lorri

May 11, 2005

Munkus dearest,

   Something has been happening to me lately. I couldn't begin to
describe it, other than to say it's magick. It reminds me of what
happened when I was sitting, only this is ten times more
overwhelming. I close my eyes and see things. You know those blue
and red circles on the Wonder Bread wrapper? I saw myself made of
tens of thousands of those, like molecules. They would separate
from me one at a time and spread out like dandelion puffs, until they
combined with something else. I was literally becoming part of
everything. I love telling you about all of this stuff, because I know
you're the only creature on earth who is capable of understanding.
Lorri, you are not a person. You really are an angel. No person could
ever be all the things that you are. You are absolutely amazing.

                                          I love you,

                                          Damien

June 21, 2005

Lovely munkus,

    Lorri, you can't ever leave me alone. I can't live without you.
Everything would be so empty and pointless. Don't you dare ever
get sick or die on me. I mean it, Lorri. Something in me starts to die
if I even think about having to make it through a day without you.
You are the fun, you are the magick, you are my life.

I am yours forever,

D.

postscript, 2014

You may have noticed that Lorri's letters and mine are becoming fewer and far between; the dates are sporadic, our moods are mercurial. By the time we reached the last few years of my incarceration, we had almost completely stopped writing to each other. Our communication had switched almost entirely to phone calls, and Lorri was visiting much more often. By the time I got out, she was living in Arkansas, so we saw each other weekly. We could talk in person about everything, and we also had the burden of casework to talk about all the time—it was Lorri's full-time job, and on some rare days, it actually felt to me like freedom was a possibility. However, more often it felt as though time had stopped; I lived in the vacuum of my cell, where days went by but nothing changed.

One of the most powerful tools within the magician's arsenal is the tarot deck. Lorri and I have used it for many years, going back to when I was in prison. It has helped us through some of the hardest times in our lives. When most people think of tarot, they think of things seen in bad horror movies and dramatic (and incorrect) television shows. They think of things like gypsy fortune-tellers whispering dramatically about crossing paths with a tall, dark stranger. In reality, nothing and no one can tell you what the future will certainly be, because we have the ability to change it at any time.

What the tarot actually does is act like a mirror that reflects our lives back to us, so that we can see things that may otherwise go unnoticed. Things such as patterns. Most of us follow patterns that we may not even be aware of. Patterns in our thinking, patterns in the way we handle our relationships, even patterns in the way we spend money. Often we can become so immersed in these patterns and routines that they become invisible to us. That's one of the many ways in which the tarot is useful. It allows us to see things with greater clarity.

When people come to me for tarot readings, I explain to them that the deck is basically divided into two kinds of cards: the major arcana and the minor arcana. *Arcana* is from an old Latin word meaning "secret"—so that tarot contains "big secrets" and "little secrets."

The major arcana, or "big secrets," are the cards people think of when they think of the tarot—cards like the Fool and the Magician. These cards point to moments in our lives that are more monumental in nature. They are road signs that mark our place on the map of spiritual evolution and growth. Not only do they point to where we are, but they also give us advice and warn us of certain pitfalls that lie at that particular fork in the road.

The minor arcana—the "little secrets"—are more about the day-to-day aspects of our lives. In the minor arcana there are four suits. There are cups, swords, wands, and pentacles. Each of these suits corresponds to a different area of our existence. The swords are all about our intellect—our ability or lack thereof to use logic and reason in different situations. The cups represent the watery aspect of ourselves—our emotions. They are about our relationships with ourselves and others, and the way we approach them. The wands represent our fiery aspect—our desire, our ambition, our creativity, and our sex drive. The pentacles represent the densest aspect of ourselves, which is the physical world—our bodies, our finances, our cars and houses and bank accounts.

There are many stories and bits of wisdom connected to each and every card. It would take an entire book to cover them all, so I'll only give a couple of examples. The first is the Hanged Man.

When I was in prison, I used to call home and talk to Lorri every single morning. One of the things we would do on that call is draw a card. We'd draw the card, and then discuss the various meanings associated with it. Once, for nearly two straight weeks, Lorri drew the Hanged Man.

The card shows a young man hanging upside down, suspended by one foot. However, despite this precarious position, he doesn't seem to be in any obvious pain or discomfort. His face is calm and serene, and there even appears to be light shining from around his head, like a halo. The Hanged Man is associated with all the old myths and stories of gods who have sacrificed themselves. Like the Christ, hanging from the cross. Or in the old Viking stories, it was Odin the All-Father, who hung from the World Tree for nine days. What all of these old stories have in common is that the central figure had to make a tremendous sacrifice, which was horrifyingly painful, but in return they gained something even more valuable. Odin gained the gifts of prophecy and magick. The Christ gained eternal life.

The moral of the Hanged Man? Nothing is free. You can have anything you want to have—but you have to pay the price. And the price is never fun. Lorri didn't enjoy seeing that card come up day after day. But we both knew that sometimes the only way out of Hell is to keep walking until you reach the other side.

For me, the Hanged Man was a reminder of my childhood wish—
the wish to be the greatest mage or magician who had ever lived. I saw
my time in prison—eighteen years and seventy-six days—as the price
I had to pay for that. The only way you become good at magick is with
practice. So the universe gave me plenty of time and opportunity to
practice, by putting me in a prison cell. It also gave me incentive—I
would be murdered by the state for something I had not done unless
I became good enough to shape a different reality.

The thing I always remember most about the Hanged Man is this:
After you've paid the price, no matter how painful, you realize it was
more than worth it.

Damien

August 4, 2005

Lovely minimus,

A man was proven innocent today after spending thirty years in prison. He went in at the age of 37. Now he's 67.

I love you, spectabalis,

D.

November 2, 2005

My lovely,

When I look inside myself now all I see is bright light. There's not even anything that people call "soul." I've gone past that. A soul is made out of mud. This light in me is pure fire. Remember when Ogden Nash said, "Where there's a monster, there's a miracle"? I know what that miracle is. It's an angel. The monster is the caterpillar, the angel is the butterfly. I would say that you are the spark that caused the big bang within me, but you are not a spark. You are the nuclear warhead. I've become a constant state of evolution. The light grows brighter and brighter. I saw this today. You have to know darkness before you can know light. Nothing else is possible. People aren't capable of understanding these things, Lorri. Their minds aren't capable of grasping it. It's no wonder they thought I was crazy.

I love you,

Damien

December 29, 2005

My dearest,

I've had so much on my mind—very, very good things. Damien, I know you willed this job for me. It's going to change my life in so many ways. I know you work hard on your book so you can help me and you have, greatly.

All the things I've been crying about over the last year, you have fixed—well, except for the one thing, and I promise I'll do that with what you are doing for me.

I am driven, now, in every way. I want so much, and I'll get it. I spent about 2 minutes today being sad because of your sad-sack letter. It's not because I don't care, it's because I'm not going to give you any reason to be sad anymore. I love you, Damien. More than I've ever loved anything in my life. I know I've made you sad over the last year (well, maybe the last ten years), but I'm going to live to make you happy. Even when you tell me annoying George Carlin jokes. You are, after all, still a boy sometimes.

But you are also one of the—no, the most amazing and wonderful man I know of.

I love you,

Lorri

Lorri,

Loving you saved my life.

Forever,
D.

Dec 31 2008

my dearest Damien, my life:

while i have never thought much of News
Years Eve, this year it is very important
to me. i will look back on a year where
i learned so much and look forward to
a year where we will accomplish so much.
of this i am certain, and excited.
I love you so much, i honor you and
look to you for guidance and inspiration
I hope you know that there is an
ocean in me, but it holds all the
colors, temperatures, scareness, and
brilliance, as well as all the 'other'
things that lurk in oceans, but it is
yours to swim in and explore,
always.
my heart is teeling with promise and love.

Your truest love,

Lou

postscript, 2014

After all of these letters here, it is astonishing—no, unbelievable—to remember that we still had three years ahead of us until Damien's release. This period of six or seven years, when we both dug in with the help of friends and supporters to really fight Damien's case, was interminable. The challenges felt insurmountable. The stress of working on the case, the permanent, never-realized physical intimacy that we both so needed—that any two people who love each other *must* have—took a terrible toll on both of us.

And yet, we made it through the years to this point, and then we made it through many more years before Damien was free. The highs and lows were extreme—one great event, like a TV show, might happen and bring attention to our cause, sparking enormous excitement and adrenaline-fueled hope. Then a year would pass: nothing. We were like soldiers coming to the end of a war; battle-scarred, fighting blindly to get through one day at a time, unaware that the end is even near. Emotionally, we were ripped to shreds.

Probably the most intense week of my life came after our lawyer

Steve Braga's call in 2011, when he told me Damien could be released in a few days' time. I went into shock, as did Damien. We were told not to tell anyone, so preparing for our next step was next to impossible. Damien started going downhill fast, and I was trying to hold him up, while working with his legal team in trying to convince Jason Baldwin to take the crazy deal the state had offered. I was allowed to tell the people closest to me, so I sought counsel from Nicole Vandenberg, Eddie Vedder, Fran Walsh, Peter Jackson, and Henry Rollins—they all gave me advice and the means to plan at least for the first year of our lives, but even then it felt like free-falling for months.

That first afternoon of freedom with Damien was the hardest. We went from the courtroom to a hotel in Memphis where everyone was having a daylong-into-evening party. Damien and I took some time in our room. For all those years of constant surveillance, here we were at last alone, and I was a little scared. Not of Damien, but of the *huge* responsibility I had. I had no idea how damaged he was from the trauma he had endured—and I wouldn't make a dent into that insight for six months. Looking back, I wonder how we made it at all. It felt like sleepwalking.

But we did, and it's just another chapter in our lives, and one from which I have once again learned how extraordinary Damien is. He has come so far in the last two years; and all I can do is look forward to what he—and we—will do next.

The last two years haven't been easy. Damien suffered from extreme PTSD, and I was lost for much of the time, trying to figure out what the next step would be, but mostly I was trying to take care of him. I was afraid he was broken, and that I would never be able to put him together again, but my Damien is extraordinary—as I have always known, as these letters attest to. He has come so far, and he is getting better every day, as am I.

I wake up sometimes wondering if we're doing the right thing for us, putting these letters, putting our lives out there for everyone to see. I had horrible fantasies that we would be taken apart for being weirdos, but after reading them, I realize it's the *only* thing I want to do right now. We lived this, and we won. We are now living the very things we wrote about; we wrote them into being, and if that doesn't speak to true, absolute magick, I don't know what else does.

I wouldn't wish this life for anyone. I would never suggest to a young woman to find a man in prison to write to, to fall in love with and to marry him. It's a brutal life for everyone involved. It breaks hearts over and over again. It is a life of deprivation that cannot be sated. I've had women write to me or ask me for advice who have found themselves in my situation—but I don't respond, because I know nothing I say will deter them. All I know, at the risk of sounding astoundingly vain, is that there will never be another situation like mine and Damien's. It was the perfect storm, so to speak—we had resources and supporters from around the world, we had actual innocence, and we somehow had the strength and love to hold on.

Looking back at the first letters and reliving everything after, I am struck with our naiveté—perhaps mine more than Damien's. He worked so hard at trying to convince me that he was all right. I was so dramatic in those first years, flying so close to the sun, not caring how far out I would venture, though in reality, it was all very close. There was just Damien and me, living in our heads and hearts, but to us it was a huge, scarily crazy adventure, because we dared to be honest with each other, and to follow whatever path our love would take us on.

I think that's the part I find hardest to read, or maybe it's comforting: We grew up. We came to a realization that in order to survive, we would have to go through searing pain. I don't even know if we realized that it was imperative to take us to the place where we would form a spiritual connection and that it would be the foundation of our relationship. Without that, the jealousies, the insecurities, and the pain we inflicted upon each other because of the insane circumstances would've eventually killed who we were. No love can survive such degradation without eventually finding a spiritual foundation, and that is what we believe and live today.

This book is our only way of showing others what it can take to keep love alive, even in the direst of circumstances. There are many people who face horrific and daunting situations. War, illness, crime—these are just some of the human conditions that cause unbelievably difficult scenarios for love. But somehow we keep finding it in all these places, and somehow we find humor and grace and humility, and even sex. Thank goodness for sex.

We will never, ever be able to fully describe what happened to us, why we found each other, and the love and perseverance it took to stay together. I just knew that once I got to know Damien, he would be my life. We still believe we will create our world, and we have many, many dreams. It's going to be a wonderful life.

As I read through these letters for the first time—it took me a while to do it, long after they had been transcribed, because I was scared— but as I read through them, I was taken back to every emotion, every longing, every painful moment, every fear. But most of all, I was made aware of what a miracle it is to have Damien with me, right now. There are times he lays his head in my lap and I stroke his hair, and I am overcome with amazement. I still walk into a room to see him and can't believe he is here with me.

Lorri

[Undated]

Lorri,

   All I know is that I've got to get the hell out of here. I've reached
the critical point. The machine is spinning full speed, and I'm
holding on so tight my hands have no blood in them. In my head I
can see one of those cartoons from the *New Yorker*—it shows Dennis
talking to a skeleton covered in spiderwebs. He's saying, "Don't
worry, the longer it takes, the better!" When I do those public talks,
people will be shocked. Liberals, defense attorneys, anti–death
penalty groups—I'll talk about them just as much as the state.
Imagine—we may not have to deal with the state at all—the judge
may just throw the whole thing out and dismiss the case. In fact, if
they can match the handprint, that's exactly what I'd bet happens.
No deals, no bargains, no trials, nothing. First stop—to get my
wedding ring sized. Second stop—the dentist. Then a long and
meandering ride wherever we want.

                                                            Damien

postscript 2014

December 31, 2013

The last day of the year, and I'm spending it on the streets of NYC. It's both a blessing and a curse. It's a blessing because there's nothing and no place in the world that is more magickal or meaningful to me. I can feel the way time has wound down and come to a grinding halt on this gray and velvety day. It has the melancholy air of something coming to an end, but also the excitement of something new beginning.

Art, art, art—my brain is alive with it these days, almost overwhelmingly so. This is one of the reasons I'm so fiercely in love with NYC. Not just that she is MY city, that she loves me and conspires with me to make tiny pockets of magick within her dark places—but the art. My God, it's everywhere. The city is saturated in it, drunk on it. From the biggest, most highbrow museums to the graffiti on every vacant wall. New York does not only inspire art—she is art. She turns life itself into a strange and glittering work of art.

Every art form in the world can be found on these streets, and every variation on that art form. For example, I have a friend named Vincent Castiglia who does giant paintings entirely in his own blood. Another friend, Jen DeNike, orchestrates performance pieces, which usually consist of naked girls doing various divination techniques.

For me, it's photography. I've come to love creating and capturing images. I'm nearly obsessed with it. I want to create dark and velvety scenarios that take the breath away. I want to use photography as my gateway into the realm of sensuality and debauchery. I want to bring every decadent desire to the forefront of the viewer's consciousness. To make them crave something more than the mundane existence they've been told they have to settle for. And New York is the perfect place—the only place—to do that. After all, the entire city is a decadent feast for the senses.

The next step I have to take is overcoming all fear. I've been out of prison about two and a half years now, yet I still experience fear on a daily basis. I've found that the only thing that breaks the walls of this internal prison is to force myself to do whatever it is that fills me with dread. Things like riding the subway by myself for the first time, or journeying into strange parts of town. The thing is, up until now I've eased into those things like an old man slipping into a tub of warm water. I can feel in my bones that those days are over. They say that fortune favors the bold. I want to find out if that's true. I want to throw myself into this life with a vengeance. I want to slam myself through all the barriers that fear has erected in my soul. My body may have left prison two and a half years ago, but my heart and soul did not. Now it's finally time for that to happen. Art will be the horse I ride to freedom.

Damien

january 2014

It's snowing again. In a matter of a couple of hours it blanketed everything. It makes the world feel so soft and quiet. I don't think I'll ever get used to it, or view it as anything less than pure magick.

A little earlier I went outside to watch it. I stood there, sending out tentacles to feel the night more than just look at it. Everything was completely silent, surrounding me like the most comforting cocoon. Lorri came over to me and asked, "What is it?"

I tried to explain it to her—how when I tell people that I imagine heaven to be a place where it's always winter, this is the energy I'm trying to convey. That to a ghost, every moment is exactly like this one. That when I am dead, this is where I will be. She just said, "I better be there."

I said, "Always."

Now I'm inside, in my safe little lair, and I feel more content than I have ever been in my life. The room is dimly lit, my tea is warm, and my pillows are as soft as clouds. All those years on death row, this is what I wished for. This is what I created in my mind to escape to, and now I have it in the physical realm. I am finally happy.

Damien

acknowledgments

To my friends Shelley Huber, Susan Wisniewski, Sherri Peacock Rebois, and Julie Althoff Bush, who believed in us from the beginning.

When I first got to Arkansas, I was taken in by Mara Leveritt and Linda Bessette. I will forever be grateful for the friendship and support you both gave us, and for all the good advice, meals, movies, and a feeling of family. I met Lucy Sauer at the prison and she taught me how to sit Zen meditation, performed our wedding, and loaned us $10,000 when the defense fund was desperate. I worked at Little Rock Parks and Recreation, and there I met Shellie Sawrey. Shellie, your friendship got me through some hard times, and you came to our wedding! I sat Zen meditation at a center in Little Rock, and there I met Mary Horne, who is still close to us to this day. Through our Saturday-night dinners I met Capi Peck, who changed my life. Capi, words can't contain the love we have for you, and no one has ever lived so well in Little Rock as I did. We had so much fun, and you gave so much of yourself to attaining Damien's freedom. David Jauss, our dear friend. Craig Stamper, thank you for the guidance and advice, but most of all for teaching me how to have the confidence to trust what I can't see. Jen DeNike, who keeps us on our toes and is a dear, sweet friend. Thank you, Randall Jamail for the excellent advice and the reassurance. Jacob Pitts: our long-lost brother, friend, and one of the loves of our lives. To Kelly Quinn, for all the rides to the prison and for caring for Tellus, Elkie, and Goswyn.

There are those of you who made my life a whole lot easier—Allen Smith, thanks for hiring me, and for letting me build my professional life around my visits with Damien. Martin Eisle, for acupuncture and friendship. Whenever I needed camera-ready hair, there was Mary Anne Britton. Thank you for all the fun times in that chair. Our book club! The Sowers, where I first learned how amazing Little Rock women were. It took finding you to bring socializing back into my life. I'm so grateful for your support. All who made up Arkansas Take Action: Our dear friends John Hardin, Rob Fisher, and Bryan Frazier, who did the unthinkable for the case, we will never forget your bravery; Claire LaFrance, Stephanie Caruthers, Holly Ballard, Tony Peck, Mike Ledford, and Mike Poe; Brent Peterson, our true friend who was always the warrior; Laird Williams; Steve Johnson; John and Laura Hardy, and countless others who made all the difference. Jim Pfieffer, our neighbor who took up the trash every week so I would have one less thing to worry about, and our accountant, Mike Johnson, thank you for everything. Our favorite Dharma teacher, Anna Cox—your persistence has created vast changes for inmates all over the country. Thank you, Emily Kern.

Then there were the thousands from around the world who donated funds and supported us in ways from which we're still reeling. In L.A.: Kathy Bakken, Chad Robertson, Burk Sauls, Grove Pashley, and Lisa Fancher ran the WM3.org website and were always there to help in any way. Damien had the opportunity to first show his art through our friend Anje Vela's efforts. Charlotte Morgan, Nick Arons, and Gita Drury brought the cause to New York and made waves. In Seattle, Kelly Canary and Danny Bland— Kelly, your friendship, support, and legal expertise helped in more ways than you know; Danny, your 2000 benefit album set us off on a path we're still on. Jene O'Keefe—always there and now helping those in similar situations in New Orleans. Nicole Vandenberg, you amaze us to this day. Your quiet determination, sage advice, and willingness to stick it out with us has been one of the gifts of our lives. Kelly Curtis, we know how much happened because you were at the helm. In Austin, Ruth and Bill Carter. Cally Salzman and Douglas Giametto in San Francisco, who are family to us and helped to fund Damien's Rule 37 hearings. Stephanie Shearer and Chris Bacorn from Denver, who are ceaselessly entertaining and brought us so much fun through their letters and visits. Ruth Carter in Virginia, the sweetest of souls.

Our core case support came from some of the most amazingly talented people living, and we have been honored to have their help and friendship. Eddie Vedder (Pearl Jam), Johnny Depp, Henry Rollins, Fran Walsh and Peter Jackson, Phillipa Boyens and Seth Miller, Margaret Cho, Natalie Maines, and Patti Smith. Then there were the hundreds of bands, artists, and writers who all contributed in countless ways.

And our legal team: amazing, amazing, amazing. Ed Mallett, thank you for your pro-bono efforts. Dennis Riordan, Don Horgan, Theresa Gibbons, and Deborah Sallings for taking on the case when it was code red and for bringing us back to life. Your briefs stunned the Arkansas Supreme Court into granting us the evidentiary hearing in 2010. The new guard who brought about the deal with the State of Arkansas that gained Damien's release: Steve Braga and Patrick Benca, with the help of Lonnie Soury and Jay Salpeter. Our investigators, Ron Lax, and Rachael Geiser, thank you for everything. John Douglas and Steve Mark for thinking outside the box. I always consider Fran Walsh a part of the legal team. A big part.

The other investigation, our documentarians and their team: Amy Berg and your tireless crew, Holly Tunkel, you were all fearless.

Post-release brought about a whole new guard who were there to hold us up, keep us safe and dry, and enabled us to charter a new life together: Jill Vedder, Danny Forster, Susie Arons, Tahra Grant, Emily Lowe Mailaender, Kevin Wilson and Liz Henderson, Sherry and Sam Chico, Lucia Coale and Ed Schutte, Brian and Lauren Consolazio, Dr. Dan and his amazing staff— Alan Russo, Julie Marsibilio, and Judith Star. Our friend and mentor Ken Kamins.

Our dear friend Michele Anthony, thank you for feeding us, housing us, and your help in healing us. A very special thanks to Joe Berlinger and Bruce Sinofsky for making *Paradise Lost*.

To our amazing, amazing team at Blue Rider Press: Sarah Hochman, the best editor in the universe; Brian Ulicky, Aileen Boyle, and David Rosenthal—thank you for believing in our story. To our literary agent,

Henry Dunow, and to our lawyer, Elliot Groffman, for your enormous generosity and big heart.

This book would not exist without Geoff Gray, who brought the idea of a story about letters to us in 2010, and Lindsey Stanberry, who transcribed thousands of our letters and gave us the loveliest of book titles. Thank you!

We suppose we've have left far too many people out, but we are so very grateful to everyone who was there for us. A shout-out to my sister Bunkey, and I want to send a special thank-you to my parents, Harry and Lynn Davis, for taking care of me, and for providing stability. Without that and God's grace, we would not have endured.

Lorri and Damien

about the authors

Damien Echols and Lorri Davis met in 1996 and were married in a Buddhist ceremony at Tucker Maximum Security Unit in Tucker, Arkansas, in 1999. Born in 1974, Echols grew up in Mississippi, Tennessee, Maryland, Oregon, Texas, Louisiana, and Arkansas. At the age of eighteen, he was wrongfully convicted of murder, along with Jason Baldwin and Jessie Misskelley, Jr., thereafter known as the West Memphis Three. Echols received a death sentence and spent almost eighteen years on death row until he, Baldwin, and Misskelley were released in 2011. The WM3 have been the subject of *Paradise Lost*, a three-part documentary series produced by HBO, and *West of Memphis*, a documentary produced by Peter Jackson and Fran Walsh. Echols is the author of the *New York Times* best-selling memoir *Life After Death* (2012) and a self-published memoir, *Almost Home* (2005).

Lorri Davis was born and raised in West Virginia. A landscape architect by training, she worked in England and New York City until relocating to Little Rock, Arkansas, in 1998. For more than a decade, Davis spearheaded a full-time effort toward Echols's release from prison, which encompassed all aspects of the legal case and forensic investigation. She was instrumental in raising funds for the defense and served as producer (with Echols) of *West of Memphis*. Echols and Davis live in New York City.